George Chalmers

An estimate of the comparative strength of Great-Britain

during the present and four preceding reigns, and of the losses of her trade from

every war since the revolution

George Chalmers

An estimate of the comparative strength of Great-Britain
during the present and four preceding reigns, and of the losses of her trade from every war since the revolution

ISBN/EAN: 9783744742078

Printed in Europe, USA, Canada, Australia, Japan

Cover: Foto ©ninafisch / pixelio.de

More available books at **www.hansebooks.com**

AN

ESTIMATE

OF THE

COMPARATIVE STRENGTH

OF ,

GREAT-BRITAIN,

DURING THE

PRESENT AND FOUR PRECEDING REIGNS;

AND OF THE

LOSSES OF HER TRADE

FROM EVERY WAR

SINCE

THE REVOLUTION.

BY

GEORGE CHALMERS.

LONDON:

PRINTED FOR JOHN STOCKDALE, OPPOSITE BURLINGTON-
HOUSE, PICCADILLY.

M.DCC.LXXXVI.

THE

P R E F A C E.

DURING the struggles of a great nation for her safety, or renown, conjunctures often arise, when the citizen, whose station does not admit of his giving advice, ought to offer his informations. The present [1782] seemed to be such a time. And the Compiler of the following sheets, having collected for a greater work various documents with regard to the national resources, thought it his duty to make an humble tender to the public of that authentic intelligence, which, amidst the wailings of despondency, had brought conviction and comfort to his own mind.

Little have they studied the theory of man, or observed his familiar life, who have not remarked, that the individual finds the highest gratification in deploring the felicities of the past, even amidst the pleasures of the present. Prompted thus by temper, he has in every age complained of its decline and depopulation, while the world was the most populous, and its affairs the most prosperous. Yet, is there reason to hope, that as found philosophy triumphs over ill-founded prejudices, the people of these islands will become less subject to the dominion of periodical apprehensions, far less to the lasting impressions of fancied misery.

The reader, who honours the following sheets with an attentive perusal, may probably find, that though we have advanced, by wide steps, during the last century, in the science of politics, we have still much to learn ; but that the summit can only be gained, by substituting accurate research for delusive speculation, and by rejecting zeal of paradox, for moderation of opinion.

A 3   Mankind

Mankind are now too enlightened to admit of confident affertion, in the place of fatisfactory proof, or plaufible novelty, for conclufive evidence. He, confequently, who propofes new modes of argument, muft expect contradiction, and he who draws novel conclufions from uncommon premifes, ought to enable the reader to examine his reafonings; becaufe it is juft inquiry, which can alone eftablifh the certainty of truth on the degradation of error. And little therefore is afferted in the following fheets, without the citation of fufficient authorities, or the mention of authentic documents, which it is now proper to explain.

As early as the reign of James I. ingenuity exerted its powers to difcover, through the thick cloud which then enveloped an interefting fubject, the value of our exports and of our imports; and thence, by an eafy deduction, to find, whether we were gainers, or lofers, by our traffic. Diligent inquirers looked into the entries at the cuftom-houfe, becaufe they knew, that a duty of five in the hundred being collected on the value of commodities, which were fent out and brought in, it would require no difficult calculation, to afcertain nearly the amount of both. And, during that reign, it was eftablifhed as a rule, not only among merchants, but ftatefmen, to multiply the general value of the cuftoms, inwards and outwards, by twenty, in order to find the true amount of the various articles, which formed the aggregate of our foreign trade.

Exceptionable as this mode was, it furnifhed, through feveral years of darknefs, the only light that our anceftors had to direct their inexperienced fteps, notwithftanding the impatience of politicians, and even the efforts of minifters. It is difficult to induce the old to alter the modes of their youth. When the committee of the privy council for trade, urged the commiffioners of the cuftoms, about the end of Charles II.'s reign,—" to enter the feveral commodities, which formed the exports and imports, to affix to each its ufual price, and to form a general total, by calculating the value of the whole,"—the cuftom-houfe officers infifted,—" that, to comply with fuch directions, would require one half of the clerks

of

of London."—And the theorists of those times continued to satisfy their curiosity, and to alarm the nation on the side of her commercial jealousy; since there existed no written evidence, by which their statements could be proved, or their declamations confuted.

It was to the liberality, no less than to the perseverance, of the House of Peers, that the public were at last indebted, in 1696, for the establishment of the Inspector-General of the Imports and Exports, and for *the Custom-house Ledger*, which contains the particulars and value of both; and which forms, therefore, the most useful record, with regard to trade, that any country possesses.

From this authentic register, the parliament was yearly supplied with details, either for argument or deliberation, and speculatists were furnished with extracts for the exercise of their ingenuity, or the formation of their projects. And it is from this commercial register, that *the value of cargoes exported*, which will be so often mentioned in this work, was also taken.

But, as actual enjoyment seldom ensures continued satisfaction, what had been demanded for a century, when it was regarded as unattainable, was ere long derided as defective, when it was possessed. And theorists, who pointed out the defects of an establishment, that could not be made perfect, found believers enow, because men's pride is gratified, by seeing imperfection in all things.

Against objectors, who thus easily found abettors, it was justly remarked, that a record, containing each specific article of our imports and exports, with the mercantile value affixed to each, would give us, as it was originally intended, by a calculation tedious yet certain, the true value of both, at least with as much exactness as a vast detail admits, or public utility demands; that it was not probably perceived, how impossible it is to set bounds to human vanity, caprice, and deceit, but, that as man, when engaged in similar pursuits, acts nearly a similar part, it was reasonable to infer, that the

fame

fame vanity, caprice, or deceit, which, in one age, incited the trader to make exaggerated entries at the custom-house, urged him, in every period, to gratify his ruling passion, when he was not carried from his bias by the dread of a forfeiture or a tax; so that the average of error, during one season, would be nearly equal to the average of error at any other epoch.

When the committee of Peers originally affixed the price, whereby each article of export and import should in future be rated, they probably knew, that the successive fluctuation of demand, arising from the change of fashion, would necessarily raise the value of some articles, and sink the price of others; but, that the same fluctuation of taste, which, in one age, occasioned an apparent error, would in the next re-establish the rule. Nor, did the Peers probably expect to ascertain the real value of the exports, or of imports, of the current year; as the prodigious extent of the calculation did not admit of a speedy deduction. But, they aimed with a laudable spirit to establish a standard, whereby a just comparison might be made, between any two given periods of the past; and thereby to infer, whether our manufactures and commerce prospered or declined, prior to the present year. This information *the Ledger of the Inspector-General* does certainly convey, with sufficient accuracy, for the uses of practice, or the speculations of theory. And, by contrasting, in the following work, the average exports of distant years, we are by this means enabled to trace the rise, the decline, or the progress of traffic, at different periods, even in every reign.

It is to the same age that we owe the establishment of *The register-general of shipping.* The original institution of this office arose from an indefinite clause in the commission of the customs, in 1703. Thus it continued incidental to the appointment of the Custom-house commissioners, till " the act for the union with Scotland requiring the then ships of Scots property to be registered in this office, it was thought fit to give it a distinct establishment, and at the same time to extend

tend

tend the account kept before of all ſhips trading over ſea, or coaſtways, in England, to the ſhips in Scotland ⁕".

The ſame reaſons, which had induced the traders to enter at the Cuſtom-houſe, in reſpect to their merchandizes, rather too much, incited them, with regard to their veſſels, to regiſter the burden rather too low, becauſe a tonnage-duty, they knew, would be often required of them at many ports : in the firſt operation they were governed by their vanity ; in the ſecond by their intereſt : and if the one furniſhes an evidence too flattering, the other gives a teſtimony too degrading. Thus have we, in the entries of the ſhipping at the Cuſtom-houſe, all the certainty that the entries of merchandize has been ſuppoſed to want. And in the following work the quantity of tonnage, rather than the number of ſhips, has been always ſtated, at different periods, with the value of cargoes, which they were ſuppoſed to tranſport, as being the moſt certain : when to the value of cargoes the tonnage is added, in the following pages, the reader is furniſhed with a ſupplemental proof to the uſeful notices, which each ſeparately convey.

Of the tonnage of veſſels, which will ſo often occur in the ſubſequent ſheets, it muſt be always remembered, that they do not denote ſo many diſtinct ſhips, which performed ſo many ſingle voyages : for, it frequently happens, that one veſſel enters and clears at the Cuſtom-houſe ſeveral times in one year, as the *colliers* of Whitehaven and Newcaſtle : but, theſe repeated voyages were in this manner always made, and will conſtantly continue ; ſo that, being always included in the annual tonnage, we are equally enabled to form a comparative eſtimate of the advance, or decline, of our navigation, at any two given epochs of the paſt. It is to be moreover remembered, that the Britiſh veſſels enter at the Cuſtom-houſe by the regiſtered tons, and not by the meaſured burden of the ſhip, which is ſuppoſed to be gene-

---

⁕ Charles Godolphin's Memorial to the Treaſury, Dec. 1717.

rally .

rally one-third more; so that the reader may in every year, through the following statements, calculate the tonnage at one-third more, than the registered tonnage has given it.

The office of inspector-general of imports and exports for Scotland, was established only in 1755. And no diligence could procure authentic details of the Scots commerce from any other source of genuine information. The blank, which appears, in the preceding period, as to the Scots traffic, sufficiently demonstrates, that imperfect evidence, with regard to an important subject, is preferable to none; as the glimmerings of the faintest dawn is more invigorating than the gloom of total opacity. Connected accounts of the shipping of Scotland cannot be given before 1759; because it is only from this year, that they have been regularly entered at the Custom-house, at least constantly kept. In respect to these, the same allowance must be made for *repeated voyages*, and the same augmentation for the *real burden* more than the *registered tonnage*.

It is not pretended, that the before-mentioned Custom-house books convey the certainty of mathematical demonstration. It is sufficient, that they contain *the best evidence which the nature of the case admits*. They have assuredly the credibility, which belongs to authentic history, though not the conviction, that is sometimes derived from the evidence of the senses. He who, in such inquiries, asks for more convincing proofs, ought to be regarded as a person, who, indulging a sceptical mind, delights to walk through the mazes of uncertainty.

The subject of population is so intimately connected with every estimate of the strength of nations, that the compiler was induced to enquire into the populousness of England, at different periods, from the earliest times to the present. In this difficult discussion, men, at once candid and able, have spoken a language, often contradictory to each other, and sometimes inconsistent with their own premises.

The

The Lord Chief Juſtice Hale, and Gregory King, in the laſt century, and Doctor Campbel and Doctor Price, in the preſent age, maintained opinions directly the reverſe of each other, in reſpect to the queſtion, Whether the people of this iſland have not gradually increaſed, during every age, or ſometimes diminiſhed, amid public convulſions and private miſery. The two firſt—the one a great maſter of the rules of evidence, the other equally ſkilful in calculation— have agreed in maintaining the affirmative of that queſtion. Doctor Campbel has laboured to ſhew, that the inhabitants of England diminiſhed in their numbers under the miſrule of feudal ſovereigns. And Doctor Price has equally contended, that the people have decreaſed, ſince a happier government was introduced at *the Revolution*, and that they continue to decreaſe.

It is propoſed to review hiſtorically the ſentiments of each, with deſign rather to aſcertain the authenticity of their facts, than to eſtabliſh, or overturn, their ſeveral ſyſtems. The candid inquirer may perhaps ſee cauſe for lamenting, in his progreſs, that the learned are ſometimes too confident, and the unlettered always too credulous. And he will have an opportunity, as he advances, of liſtening to the ſentiments of his anceſtors, on various topics of legiſlation, and of obſerving the condition of different ranks of men, previous to the period, at which THIS ESTIMATE properly begins.

E

C

give
way
the
fitio
T
Jam
fider
tural
moti
ward
It
luftr
it is
lates
beho
fea,
whic
the

ESTIMATE, &c.

OF the exifting numbers of mankind, in fucceffive ages of the world, various writers have
given diffimilar accounts, becaufe they did not always acknowledge the fame facts, or often adopt
the fame principles, in their moft ingenious difqui-
fitions.

The Lord Chief Juftice Hale formerly, and Sir
James Stuart and the Count de Buffon lately, confidered men, as urged, like other animals, by natural inftincts; as directed, like them, by the fame
motives of propagation; and as fubfifted afterwards, or deftroyed, by fimilar means.

It is inftinct then, which, according to thefe illuftrious authors, is the caufe of procreation; but
it is food, that keeps population full, and accumu-
lates numbers. The force of the firft principle we
behold in the multitudes, whether of the fifh of the
fea, the fowls of the air, or the beafts of the field,
which are yearly produced: we perceive however
the effential confequence of the laft, from the vaft
numbers that annually perifh for want.

B   Experience

Experience indeed evinces, to what an immenfe extent domeftic animals may be multiplied, by providing abundance of food. In the fame manner, mankind have been found to exift and increafe, in every condition, and in every age, according to the ftandard of their fubfiftence, and to the meafure of their comforts.

Hence Mr. Hume juftly concludes, that if we would bring to fome determination the queftion concerning the populoufnefs of ancient and modern times, it will be requifite to compare the *domeftic* and *political* fituations of the two periods, in order to judge of the facts by their moral caufes; becaufe, if every thing elfe be equal, it feems reafonable to expect, that where there are the wifeft inftitutions, and the moft happinefs, there will alfo be the moft people.

Let us run over the hiftory of England, then, with a view to thefe reafonings and to thefe facts.

Settled probably about a thoufand years before the birth of Chrift, England was found, on the arrival of Cæfar, to contain a *great multitude of people.* But this *royal and noble author* tranfmitted notices, with regard to the modes of life, which prevailed among thofe whom he came to conquer, whence we may judge of their numbers with greater certainty, than from the accuracy of his language, or the weight of his authority. And he fubmits to our judgment fufficient *data*, when he informs us, that the inhabitants of the inland country fubfifted by feeding of flocks, while their

neighbours

neighbours, along the shores of the ocean were maintained by the more productive labours of agriculture.

Having already arrived, some of the tribes in the second, and others of them in the third stage of society, in its progress to refinement, the Britons were soon taught the arts of manufacture, and the pursuits of commerce, by their civilizing conquerors. A people who annually employed eight hundred vessels to export the surplus produce of their husbandry, must have exerted great industry at home, and enjoyed sufficient plenty from it. Roman Britain, of consequence, must have become extremely populous, during that long period, from the arrival of the Romans, 55 years before the birth of Christ, to the abdication of their government, in 446 of our æra[*].

From this event commenced a war of six hundred years continuance, if we calculate the settlement of the Saxons, the ravages of the Danes, and the conquest of the Normans. A course of hostilities, thus lengthened beyond example, and wasteful beyond description, changed completely the political situation of the people, by involving them in ages of wretchedness. It was to these causes owing, that the inhabitants became divided, at the epoch of *The Conquest*, into five several classes; the barons, the free tenants, the free soccagers, together with the villains and the slaves, who formed the great body of the people [†].

[*] Mr. Whitaker's History of Manchester.   [†] Id.

A con-

'A confideration of the foregoing events, it probably was, with the wretched condition of every
order of men, which induced the Lord Chief
Juftice Hale and Mr. Gregory King to agree in
afferting *, " that the people of England, at the
" arrival of the Normans, might be fomewhat
" above *two million.*" And the notices of that
moft inftructive record, the Domefday Book, feem
to juftify the conjectures of both, by exhibiting
fatisfactory proofs of a very fcanty population in
the country, as well as in the towns.

The annals of England, from the epoch of the
Conqueft to the date of the Great Charter (from
1066 to 1215) are filled with revolutions in the
government, and infurrections of the people;
with domeftic war and foreign ravages; with frequent famines, and their attendant peftilence.

Doctor Campbel has enumerated ‡ various circumftances to demonftrate the unhappinefs of the
nation, during thofe times, equally ferocious and
unfettled; and, by neceffary confequence, the
conftant decline of their numbers.

Few revolutions, faid he, even when achieved
by the moft wafteful conquerors, appear to have
been attended with fo fudden a revolution, both
of property and of power, as that which William I. unhappily introduced into England.
The conftitution, from being limited and free,
became at once arbitrary and fevere. While the

* Origination of Mankind; and Davenant's Works.
‡ Political Survey,

ancient

ancient nobility feemed to be annihilated, the
Saxon people were affuredly reduced to villainage. And thofe revolts enfued fucceffively, which neceffarily arife, when a gallant people are defpifed, at the fame time, that they are
oppreffed. The Conqueror, urged partly by re-
venge, perhaps more by policy, was provoked, by
the infurrection of the northern counties, to pre-
fcribe remedies as fevere as they were barbarous.
He fo effectually depopulated the extenfive country from *the Humber* to *the Tees*, that it lay for
years uncultivated, whereby multitudes perifhed
for want. The pleafures of *William* too were as
deftructive to the people as his anger. In forming the New Foreft, he laid wafte an extent of
thirty miles in Hampfhire, without regarding the
cries of villagers, or the facrednefs of churches.
And his gratitude to his fupporters, though attended with lefs violence, produced, in the end, confequences ftill more fatal, with regard to the depopulation of England, than had refulted either from
his refentment, or his fport. He diftributed the
whole kingdom to about feven hundred of his
principal officers, who afterwards divided among
their followers the fpoils of the vanquifhed, on
fuch precarious tenures as fecured the fubmiffion
of the lower orders, though not their happinefs.

The Conqueror's meafures, thus harfhly execut-
ed, continued to influence all ranks of men, long
after the terrors of his government had ceafed ;
and while they neither fecured the quiet, nor pro-

B 3   moted

moted the plenty of the nation, his rigours probably added very few to its numbers.

The great charter of John made no alteration in public law, or any innovation in private rights: and though it conferred additional security on the free, it gave little freedom to the slave. Yet, the barbarous licence both of kings and nobles being thenceforth somewhat restrained, government, says Mr. Hume, approached by degrees nearer to that end for which it was instituted, the equal protection of every order in the state.

This general reasoning, however just, did not impose on the sagacity of Doctor Campbel, who minutely examined every circumstance in our subsequent annals, that tended either to retard or promote an effective population. He found no event in the long reign of Henry III. filled as it was with distraction, proceeding from weaknefs, and with civil war, the refult of turbulence, which could have added one man to our numbers. Though historians have celebrated the following reigns of our Edwards, as the moft glorious in our annals; yet he remarked, that, during a period wherein there were fcarcely ten years of peace, the eclat of victories, the splendour of triumphs, or the acquifition of diftant territories, did not compenfate the lofs of inhabitants, who continually decreafed, from the wafte of foreign and civil wars, and from the debility of peftilential diftempers, arifing from a wretched hufbandry, as much as from a noxious ftate of the atmofphere. It was a

shrewd

shrewd remark of Major Graunt, when he was re-
flecting over "*the sickliness, the healthfulness, and fruit-*
"*fulness of seasons,*" that "*the more sickly the years*
"*are, the less fruitful of children they also be.*"

The first notice, which the Parliament seem to
have taken of the paucity of inhabitants, may be
seen in the *Statute of Labourers,* that was enacted in
1349. This law recites—"That whereas a great
part of the people, and especially of workmen and
servants, late died of the pestilence, many, seeing
the necessity of masters and great scarcity of servants, will not serve, unless they receive excessive
wages, some being rather willing to beg in idleness, than by labour to get their living." Consi-
dering therefore " the grievous incommodities
which of the lack, especially of ploughmen and
such labourers, may hereafter come," Edward III.
with the assistance of the *prelates,* the *nobles,* and
the *learned men,* ordained a variety of regulations,
unjust in their theory, and violent in their execution *. This edict of the King in council was enforced

---

* These regulations may be seen in Cay's Collection of
Statutes, vol. i. p. 261—3 ; and sufficiently evince to what a
deplorable state of slavery the collective mass of the people was
then reduced. " Every able-bodied person, under sixty years
of age, not having sufficient to live on, being required, shall
be bound to serve him that doth require him, or else shall be
committed to gaol, till he finds security to serve. If a servant,
or workman, depart from service before the time agreed upon,
he shall be imprisoned. If any artificer take more wages than
were wont to be paid, he shall be committed to gaol." The

severity

forced by the legiflature in the fubfequent year—
" on the petition of the commonalty, that the faid
fervants, having no regard to the faid ordinance,
but to their eafe and fingular covetife, do with-
draw to ferve great men and other, *unlefs they have
wages and living to the double and treble of that they
were wont to take the twentieth year of the king that
now is.*"

Yet, after adjufting minutely the prices of labour, of natural products, and even of manufactures, the ftatute of the 23d Edward III. directed,
" that the artificers fhould be fworn to ufe their
crafts as they did in the twentieth year of the fame
king * " (1346), under the penalty of imprifon-
ment, at the difcretion of the Juftices. The Parliament bufied themfelves, year after year, in re-
gulating labour, which had been defrauded of its
juft reward, by confiderable defalcations from the
coin †. During an adminiftration lefs active, and
vigorous,

---

feverity of thefe penalties was foon greatly increafed by the
34th Edward III. which directs, " That if any labourer or
fervant flee to any town, the chief officer fhall deliver him
up: and if they depart to another county, they fhall be
burnt in the forehead with the letter F." Thus, fays Anderfon, they lived, till manufactures drove flavery away.
Chron. Ac. of Com. v. i. p. 204.

* Chap. 1—7.

† From the value of *the pound,* or twenty fhillings in prefent money, as eftablifhed by Edward I. in 1300, there were
deducted by Edward III. in the 18th of his reign, 4s. 11d. ¼,
and in the 20th of his reign 9d. ¼ more; fo that there had
been

vigorous, and respected, than Edward's, such regulations had produced tumult and revolt. Scarce-
ly indeed was that great monarch laid in his grave,
when the confirmation of the same statutes, by his
feeble successor, gave rise to the memorable rebellion of Tyler and Straw, so destructive in its immediate effects, so beneficial in its ultimate consequences! The common people acquired im-
plied liberty from insurrection, while the Parliament were enacting *, " *that forced manumissions
should be confidered as void.*" And such are the revolutions, which infenfibly take place, during ages
of darkness, before the eyes of chroniclers, who
are carried away by the sound of words, without
regarding the efficacy of things.

The declamatory recitals of such statutes ought
generally to be regarded as flight proofs of the
authenticity of facts, unless where they are fupported by collateral circumstances. From the re-
iterated debasement of the coin, which proceeded
from the expensive wars of Edward III. we might
be apt to infer, that the recited destruction of the
pestilence was merely a pretence to palliate motives of avarice, or to justify the rigours of op-
pression.

On the other hand, Doctor Mead assures us,
that the greatest mortality, which has happened in

been taken no less than five shillings and nine pence from the
standard pound, settled in 1300, of £.2. 17s. 5d.
Harris on Coins, part ii. ch. i.

* By the 5th Richard II.

4   later

later ages, was about the middle of the four-
teenth century; when the plague that feized England, Scotland, and Ireland, in 1349, *is faid* to
have difpeopled the earth of *more than half* of its
inhabitants [*]. The Commons petitioned, during
the Parliament [†] of 1364, that, in confideration
of the preceding peftilence, the King would allow
perfons, who held lands of him in chief, to let
leafes without a licence, as had been lately practifed, *till the country were become more populous.*
From the 23d of Edward I. when the cities and
boroughs are faid to have been firft formally fum-
moned to Parliament, to the demife of Edward IV.
the fheriffs often returned, *That there were no
cities or boroughs in their counties, whence reprefenta-
tives could be fent.* This form of expreffion Doctor Brady [‡] has very juftly explained to mean,
That the towns were fo depopulated and poor,
as to be unable to pay the accuftomed expences
of delegates. The truth of this reprefentation,
and of this commentary, is indeed confirmed by
a law of Henry VII. [§]; which recites, That
where, in fome towns, two hundred perfons lived
by their lawful labours, now they are occupied by
two or three herdfmen, and the refidue fall into

[*] Difcourfe concerning Peft. Contag. p. 24—5.
[†] Cott. Abr. of Records, p. 97.
[‡] Of Boroughs, p. 125, &c.
[§] 4th Henry VII. ch. 19; which is publifhed in the Appendix to Pickering's Statutes, vol. xxiii.

idlenefs.

idleness. And from the foregoing facts we may
surely infer, that there must have been a great paucity of people in England, during those *good old
times*, at least towards the conclusion of the celebrated reign of Edward III.

From incontrovertible evidence we can now
establish the whole number of inhabitants, with sufficient exactness to answer all the practical pur-
poses of the statesman, and even to satisfy all the
scrupulous doubts of the sceptic. A poll-tax of
four pence having been imposed by the Parliament of the 51st of Edward III. (1377) on every
lay person, as well male as female, of *fourteen* years
and upwards, real mendicants only excepted, an
official return of the persons who paid the tax, in
each county, city, and town, has been happily preserved [*]. And from this *subsidy-roll* it appears,

---

[*] This record, so instructive as to the state of England at
the demise of Edward III. was laid before the Antiquary Society, in December 1784, by Mr. Topham of the Paper-
Office; a gentleman, whose curious research with regard to
the jurisprudence and history of his country, as well as com-
municative disposition, merits the greatest praise. Mr. Topham observed, that the sum collected, in consequence of the
subsidy of 1377, being £.22,607. 2s. 8d. contained only
1,356,428 groats, which ought to have been the amount of
those who were fourteen years of age and upwards. But I
have chosen to state the number of persons, who are mentioned
in the roll as having paid, in each county and town, amounting to 1,367,239, though the total mistakingly added on the
record is 1,376,442.

that

that the *lay* perſons who paid this tax amounted
to ‑ ‑ ‑ 1,367,239.
When we have aſcertained what proportion the
perſons paying bore to *the whole*, we ſhall be able
to form a ſufficient eſtimate of the total population. It appears from the Table formed by Doctor Halley, according to the Breſlaw births and
burials; from the Northampton Table; from the
Norwich Table; and from the London Table,
conſtructed by Mr. Simpſon; as theſe Tables are
publiſhed by Doctor Price *, That the perſons at
any time living *under* fourteen years of age are a
good deal fewer than *one third* of the co-exiſting
lives. And the *lay* perſons, who paid the tax in
1377, muſt conſequently have been a *good deal
more* than *two thirds* of the whole.

But, ſince there may have been omiſſions of the perſons paying ‑ 1,367,239
Add one third ‑ ‑ ‑ ‑ 455,746
                                  ─────────
                                  1,822,985

Add the number of beneficed clergy
  paying the tax ‑ ‑ 15,229
And the non‑beneficed
  clergy ‑ ‑ ‑ ‑ 13,932
                              ───────
                                       29,161
                              ─────────
                                  1,852,146

* Obſerv. on Reverſ. Payments, vol. ii. p. 35—6, 39—40.

But

But Wales, not being included in this
roll, is placed on a footing with
Yorkſhire *, at   -   -   -   174,720
Cheſhire and Durham, having had their
own receivers, do not appear on the
roll ; the firſt is ranked with Corn-
wall, at   -   -   -   -   -   45,700
The ſecond with Northumberland, at   20,412
                                    ─────────
The whole people of England and
Wales   -   -   -   2,092,978
                                    ─────────

We can now build upon a rock ; having before
us proofs almoſt equal in certainty to actual enumerations. Yet what a picture of public miſrule,
and private miſery, does the foregoing ſtatement
diſplay, during an unhappy period of three hun-

* From Davenant's Table (in his Eſſay on Ways and
Means, p. 76.) it appears, that Wales paid a much ſmaller
ſum to the poll-tax of the 1ſt of William and Mary, to the
quarterly poll, and indeed to every other tax, and contained
a much lower number of houſes, according to the hearth-books
of Lady-day 1690. It was giving a very large allowance to
Wales, when this country was placed on an equality with
Yorkſhire, which paid, in 1377, for 131,040 lay perſons.
The population of Cheſhire and Durham was ſettled upon ſimilar principles ; and is equally ſtated in the text at a medium rather too high. So that, as far as we can credit this
authentic record, in reſpect to the whole number of lay perſons upwards of fourteen years of age, we muſt believe, that
this kingdom contained at the demiſe of Edward III. about
TWO MILLIONS, one hundred thouſand ſouls ; making a rea-
ſonable allowance for the uſual omiſſions of taxable perſons.

dred

dred years.! We here behold the powerful operation of those causes of depopulation, which Doctor Campbel collected, in order to support his hy-
pothesis of a decreasing population, in *feudal times*.
But were we to admit that one half of the people
had been carried off by the desolating plague of
1349, as Doctor Mead supposes; or even one
third, as Mr. Hume represents with greater probability; we should find abundant reason to ad-
mire the solidity of Lord Hale's argument, in favour of a progressive population; because this
circumstance would alone evince, that there had
been, during that long effluxion of time, a considerable increase of numbers, in different ages of
tranquillity or of healthiness. A comparison too
of the notices of Domesday Book with the statements of the Subsidy Roll, would shew a much
inferior populousness soon after the Conquest in
1077, than at the demise of Edward III. in 1377.

We

We fhall find additional proofs, perhaps fome amufement, from taking a view of our principal towns, as they were found, and are reprefented by the tax-gatherers, in 1377.

London paid for - 23,314 lay perfons ; and
  contained confequently about - 33,000 fouls.
Weftminfter for - 7,389 - 10,000
York for - - 7,248 - 10,000
Briftol for - - 6,345 - 9,000
Plymouth for - 4,837 - 6,500
Coventry for - 4,817 - 6,500
Norwich * for - 3,952 - 5,300
Lincoln for - 3,412 - 4,600
Sarum (Wilts) for 3,226 - 4,400
Lynn for - - 3,127 - 4,200
Colchefter for - 2,955 - 4,000
Beverley for - 2,663 - 3,600
Newcaftle on Tyne for 2,647 - 3,600
Canterbury for - 2,574 - 3,500
St. Edmondfbury for 2,442 - 3,300
Oxford for - 2,357 - 3,200
Glocefter for - 2,239 - 3,000
Leicefter for - 2,101 - 3,000
Salop for - - 2,082 - 3,000

* Dr. Price talks of Norwich having been a great city formerly. The Domefday Book fhews fufficiently the diminu-
tivenefs of our towns in 1077 : and Mr. Topham's Subfidy
Roll puts an end to conjecture with regard to the populoufnefs of any of them anterior to 1377.

Thefe

Thefe are the only towns, which then paid the poll-tax of a groat for more than two thoufand lay per-fons, of fourteen years of age and upwards. And their inconfiderablenefs evinces a marvellous depo-pulation in the country, and a lamentable want of manufactures and commerce every where in Eng-land. Yet, Domefday Book reprefents our cities to have been little fuperior to villages at the Con-queft *; and ftill more inconfiderable than they certainly were at the demife of Edward III.

The informations of contemporary writers would, neverthelefs, lead us to confider thofe ear-ly reigns as times of overflowing populoufnefs. Amidft all that depopulation, Edward III. is faid to have fuddenly collected, in 1360, a hundred thoufand men, whom he tranfported in eleven hundred veffels to France†. It did not, how-ever, efcape the fagacity of Mr. Hume, when he reflected on the high pay of the foldiers, that the numerous armies mentioned by the hiftorians of thofe days, confifted chiefly of raggamuffins, who followed the camp for plunder. In 1382, the re-bels, fays Daniel ‡, fuddenly marched towards London, under Wat. Tyler and Jack Straw, and muftered on Blackheath fixty thoufand ftrong, or, as others fay, an hundred thoufand. In 1415, Henry V. invaded France with a fleet of fixteen hundred fail ‖, and fifty thoufand combatants, who

* See Brady on Boroughs.
† Ander. Chron. Ac. of Com. v. i. p. 191.
‡ Hiftory of Richard, in Kennet, p. 245.
‖ And. Chron. Ac. of Com. v. i. p. 245.

not

not long after won the glorious battle of Azin-
court. Hiftory is filled with fuch inftances of
vaft armies, which had been haftily levied for temporary enterprizes : yet, we ought not thence to
infer, that the country was overftocked with inhabitants. The ftatute of the 9th Henry V. recites, " That whereas, at the making of the act of
" the 14th of Edward III. (1340) there were fuf-
" ficient of proper men in each county to execute
" every office ; but that, owing to peftilence and
" wars, there are not now (1421) a fufficiency of
" refponfible perfons to act as fheriffs, coroners,
" and efcheators." The laurels which were gained
by Henry V. are well known, fays the learned ob-
ferver on the ancient ftatutes ; but he hath left us,
in the preamble of one of his ftatutes, moft irre-
fragable proof, that they were not obtained, but
at the deareft price, *the depopulation of the country*.

The facility with which great bodies of men
were collected, in thofe early ages, exhibits then, for
our inftruction, a picture of manners, idle and li-
centious ; and fhews only, for our comfort, that the
moft numerous claffes of mankind exifted in a
condition, which is not to be envied by thofe, who,
in better times, enjoy either health or eafe.

The period from the acceffion of Henry IV. in
1399, to the proclamation of Henry VII. in 1485,
may be regarded as the moft difaftrous in our latter
annals ; becaufe, a civil war, remarkable for the in-
veteracy of the leaders, and for the wafte of the
people, began with the one event, and ended with

C   the

the other. Doctor Campbel has collected the *various circumstances of depopulation*; tending to prove, that the number of inhabitants, which, before the bloody contests between the Lancastrians and Yorkists began, had been already much lessened, was in the end greatly reduced, by a series of the most destructive calamities. The monuments of more settled times were demolished; the country was laid waste; cities sunk into towns, while towns dwindled into villages; and universal desolation is said to have ensued. If, indeed, we could implicitly credit the recitals of the laws of Henry VII. we should find sufficient evidence, " That great desolations daily do increase, by pull- " ing down and wilful waste of houses and towns, " and by laying to pasture lands which customably " have been used in tillage."

An important change had certainly taken place mean while, in the condition of the great body of the people, which fortunately promoted their happiness, and which consequently proved favourable to the propagation of the species.

There existed in England, at the Conquest, no *free hands*, or freemen, who worked for wages; since the scanty labour of times, warlike and unindustrious, was wholly performed by villains, or by slaves. The latter, who composed a very numerous class, equally formed an object of foreign trade, for ages after the arrival of the Conqueror, who only prohibited the sale of them to infidels*.

* Dr. Henry's History of Great Britain.

But

But *the flaves* had happily departed from the land before the reign of Henry III. This we may infer from the law declaring, in 1225, " *How men* " *of all forts fhall be amerced* * :" and it only mentions villains, freemen, (though probably not in the modern fenfe), merchants, barons, earls, and men of the church. Another order of men is alluded to rather than mentioned, during the fame feffion; whom we fhall find, in after times, rifing to great importance, from their numbers and opulence. And a woollen manufacture, having already increafed to that ftage of it when frauds begin, was regulated by the act †, which required, " *There fhall be but one meafure throughout the* " *realm.*"

Yet this manufacture continued inconfiderable during the warlike reign of Edward I. and the turbulent adminiftration of his immediate fuccefsor, if we may judge from the vaft exportations of wool.

The year 1331 marks the firft arrival of Walloon manufacturers, when Edward III. wifely determined to invite foreigners into England ‡, to inftruct his fubjects in the ufeful arts. As early as the Parliament of 1337, it was enacted, That no wool fhould be exported; that no one fhould wear any but Englifh cloth ; that no clothes made beyond feas fhould be imported; that foreign clothworkers might come into the king's domi-

* 9 Henry III. ch. 14.   † 9 Henry III. ch. 25.
‡ And. Chron. Ac. of Com. v. i. p. 162.

. nions,

nions, and fhould have fuch franchifes as might fuffice them.

Before this time, fays De Wit *, when the tumults of the manufacturers in Flanders obliged them to feek fhelter in other countries, the Englifh were little more than fhepherds and wool-fellers. From this epoch manufactures became often the object of legiflation, and the fpirit of induftry will be found to have influenced greatly the ftate of population.

The ftatutes of labourers of 1349 and 1350 demonftrate a confiderable change in the condition and purfuits of the moft numerous claffes. During feveral reigns after the Conqueft, men laboured, becaufe they were flaves. For fome years before thefe regulations of the price of work, men were engaged to labour, from a fenfe of their own freedom, and of their own wants. It was the ftatutes of labourers †, which, adding the compulfion of law to the calls of neceffity, created oppreffion for ages, while they ought to have given relief. It is extremely difficult to afcertain the time when villainage ceafed in England, or even to trace its decline. The Edwards, during the preffure of their foreign conquefts, certainly manumitted many of their villains for money. Owing

* Intereft of Holland.
† See the 12th Richard II. ch. 3, 4, 5, 6, 9. By thefe, no artificer, labourer, fervant, or victualler, fhall depart from one hundred to another, without licence under the king's feal. Thefe laws, fays Anderfon, are fufficient proofs of the flavifh condition of the common fervants in thofe times (1388).

3

to the previous fewnefs of inhabitants, the numerous armies, which for almoft a century defolated
the nation amidft our civil wars, muft have been
neceffarily compofed of the lower ranks: and we
may reafonably fuppofe, that the men, who had
been brought from the drudgeries of flavery to
contend as foldiers, for the honour of nobles and
the rights of kings, would not readily relinquifh
the honourable fword for the meaner ploughfhare.
The church, even in the darkeft ages, remonftrated
againft the unchriftian practice of holding fellow-
men in bondage. The courts of juftice did not
willingly enforce the mafter's claim to the fervi-
tude of his villains, till, in the progrefs of knowledge, intereft difcovered, that the purchafed labour of freemen was more productive than the
liftlefs and ignoble toil of flaves. Owing to thefe
caufes, there were certainly few villains in England at the acceffion of Henry VII.* ; and the
great body of the people having thus gained greater
freedom, and with it greater comfort, thenceforth
acquired the numerous bleffings, which every where
refult from an orderly adminiftration of eftablifhed
government.

During almoft a century, before the acceffion of
Henry VII. in 1485, the manufacturers of wool,

* The ftatute of 23 Henry VI. chap, 12. mentions only fervants, artificers, workmen, and labourers; and there is a
diftinction made between hufbandry fervants and domeftic
fervants. Yet villains are fpoken of, even in our courts of
juftice, though feldom, as late as the time of James I.

with

with their attendant artificers, had fixed the feat of
their induftry, in every county in England. The
principle of the act of navigation had been introduced
into our legiflation, as early as 1381, by
the law declaring *, " That none of the king's
" fubjects fhall carry forth, or bring merchandizes,
" but only in fhips of the king's allegiance." The
fifheries too had been encouraged †. Agriculture
had been moreover promoted, by the law
which declared ‡, " That all the king's fubjects
" may carry corn out of the realm when they
" will." And *guilds, fraternities*, and *other companies*,
having foon after their creation impofed monopolizing
reftraints, were corrected by a law of
Henry VI. § ; though our legiflators were not very
fteady, during an unenlightened age, in the application
of fo wife a policy.

In reading the laws of Edward IV. we think
ourfelves in modern times, while the fpirit of the
mercantile fyftem was in its full vigour, before it
had been fo perfpicuoufly explained and fo ably exploded ‖.
It is however in the laws ** of Richard
III. that we fee more clearly the commercial ftate
of England, during the long period, wherein the
Englifh people were unhappily too much engaged
in *king-making*. In *thefe* inaufpicious times was

* 5 Richard II. ch. 3.—6 Richard, ch. 8.
† By 6 Richard II. ch. 11, 12.
‡ 17 Richard II. ch. 7.
§ 15 Hen. VI. ch. 6.
‖ By Dr. Smith's Effay on the Wealth of Nations.
** 1 Richard III. ch. 6, 8, 9, 11, 12, 13.

the

the trade of England chiefly carried on by Italians, at leaft by merchants from the fhores of the Mediterranean. The manufacturers were compofed moftly of Flemings, who, under the encouragement of Edward III. had fled from the diftractions of the Netherlands, for repofe and employment in England. And the perufal of the preamble of one of Richard's laws *, will furnifh a convincing proof of this: " Moreover, a great num-
" ber of artificers and other ftrangers, not born
" under the king's obeifance, do daily refort to
" London, and to other cities, boroughs, and
" towns, and much more than they were wont to
" do in times paft, and inhabit by themfelves in
" this realm, with their wives, children, and
" houfehold; and will not take upon them any la-
" borious occupation, as going to plough and cart,
" and other like bufinefs, but ufe the making of
" cloth, and other handicrafts and eafy occupa-
" tions; and bring from the parts beyond the fea
" great fubftance of wares and merchandizes to
" fairs and markets, and other places, at their
" pleafure, to the impoverifhment of the king's
" fubjects; and will only take into their fervice
" people born in their own countries; whereby
" the king's fubjects, for lack of occupation, fall
" into idlenefs and vicious living, to the great per-

* 1 Richard III. ch. 9. But Henry VII., *upon the fuppli-
cation of the Italian merchants,* repealed the greater part of this
law, which impofed reftraints on *aliens*; yet retained the for-
feitures incurred, in the true fpirit of his avaricious government.

C 4 " turbance

" turbance of the realm."—All this was directed otherwife by Henry VII. though probably without much fuecefs, " upon the petition made of " the Commons of England." In the prefent times, it is perhaps the wifeft policy, *neither to encourage foreigners to come, nor to drive them away.*

When manufacturers have been thoroughly fettled, nothing more is wanting to promote the wealth and populoufnefs of a country from their labour, than the protection of their property and freedom, by the impartial adminiftration of juftice; while their frauds are repreffed, and their combinations prevented, by doing equal right to every order in the ftate.

The policy of Henry VII. has been praifed by hiftorians fully equal to its worth. Anderfon relates [*], that this prince, " finding the woollen ma-" nufactures declining, drew over fome of the beft " Netherland clothmakers, as Edward III. had " done 150 years before." This is probably faid without authority; fince the law of the preceding reign, concurring with the temper of the times, did not permit the eafy execution of fo unpopular a meafure. Henry VII. like his two immediate predeceffors, turned the attention of the Parliament to agriculture and manufacture, to commerce and navigation, becaufe he found the current of the national fpirit already running toward all thefe falutary objects : hence, fays Bacon, it was no hard matter to difpofe and affect the Parliament

* Chron. Atc. of Com. v. i. p. 306.

in

in this bufinefs. And the legiflature enacted a variety of laws, which that illuftrious hiftorian explains, with his ufual perfpicuity *; all tending, fays he, in their wife policy, *towards the population apparently*, *and the military forces of the realm certainly*.

That monarch's meafures for breaking the oppreffive power of the nobles; for facilitating the alienation of lands; *for keeping within reafonable bounds the bye-laws of corporations*; and, above all, for fuppreffing the numerous bodies of men, who were then retained in the fervice of the great; all thefe deferve the higheft commendation, becaufe they were attended with effects, as lafting as they were efficacious.

It may be however doubted, whether his piddling hufbandry of petty farms, which has been oftentatioufly praifed by Doctor Price, can produce a fufficiency of food for a manufacturing country, or even prevent the too frequent returns of famine. Agriculture muft be practifed as a trade, before it can fupply fuperabundance. Certain it is †, however, that till the reign of Henry VIII. we had in England no carrots, turnips, cabbages, or fallads; and few of the fruits, which now ornament our gardens, or exhilarate our tables.

The fpirit of improvement, however, which had taken deep root, before the acceffion of Henry VIII. continued to fend forth vigorous fhoots dur-

* Hiftory in Kennet, v. i. p. 504—7.
† And. Chron. Com. v. i. p. 338.

ing

ing his reign. This we might infer from the frequent proclamations against the practice of inclosing, which was said to create *a decay of husbandry*. On the other hand, a statute was enacted to enforce the sowing of flax-seed and hemp. The nation is represented *to have been over-run by foreign manufacturers*, whose superior diligence and œconomy occasioned popular tumults. While the kingdom was gradually filling with people, it was the yearly practice to grant money to repair towns, which were supposed to be falling into ruins. Yet the numerous laws, that were enacted by the Parliaments of Henry VIII. for the paving of streets in various cities and villages, evince how much industry had gained ground of idleness ; how much opulence began to prevail over penury ; and how far a desire of comfort had succeeded to the languors of sloth. Thus much might indeed be discovered, from the numerous laws, which were during this period passed, for giving a monopoly of manufacture to different towns ; and which prove, that a great activity prevailed, by the frequent desire of selfish enjoyment, contrary to the real interest of the tradesmen themselves.

The statute, however, which limited the interest of money to 10 *per cent.* demonstrates, that much *ready money* had not yet been brought into the coffers of lenders ; while a greater number of borrowers desired to augment their wealth, by employing the money of others in the operations of trade. The kings of England, both before and

after

after this epoch, borrowed large fums in Genoa
and the Netherlands. A parliamentary debate of
the year 1523, exhibits a lively picture of the opinions that were at this time entertained as to *circulation*, which, in modern times, has fo great an
effect on the ftrength of nations. A fupply of
eight hundred thoufand pounds being afked by
Cardinal Wolfey for the French war, Sir Thomas More, the Speaker of the Commons, endeavoured to convince *the Houfe, That it was not much,
on this occafion, to pay four fhillings in the pound.*
But to this the Commons objected, That though
true it was fome perfons were well monied, yet,
in general, the fifth part of men's goods was not
in plate or money, but in ftock or cattle; and that
to pay away all their coin would alter the whole
intercourfe of things, and there would be a ftop
in all traffick; and confequently the fhipping of
the kingdom would decay. To this grave objection it was however gravely anfwered, That the
money ought not to be accounted as loft, or taken
away, but only as transferred into other hands of
their kindred or nation; fo that no more was about
to be done than we fee ordinarily in markets,
where, though the money change mafters, yet
every one is accommodated. Nor need you fear
this fcarcenefs of money; the intercourfe of things
being fo eftablifhed throughout the world, *that
there is a perpetual circulation of all that can be neceffary to mankind.* Thus your commodities will
ever find out money; while our own merchants
will

will be as glad of your corn and cattle, as you can be of any thing they can bring you[*].

Such is the argument of Sir Thomas More; who has thus left a proof to posterity of how much he knew, with regard to modern œconomy, without the aid of modern experience. No one at present can more clearly explain the marvellous accommodation of money, when quickly passed from hand to hand, or the great facility in raising public supplies, when every one can easily convert his property, either fixed or moveable, into the metals, which are the commodious measure of all things. And this is *circulation*, of which we shall hear so much in later times; and which creates so momentous a strength, when it exists in full vigour; yet leaves, when it disappears, so great a debility.

But the suppression of monasteries, and the reformation of religion, are the measures of Henry VIII.'s reign, which were attended with consequences the most happy and the most lasting. Fifty thousand persons are said to have been maintained in the convents of England and Wales, who were thus forced into the active employments of life. And a hundred and fifty thousand persons are equally supposed to have been restrained from marriage†, which can alone produce effective population.

---

[*] Lord Herbert's History of Henry VIII. in Kennet, v. ii. p. 55.

† And. Chron. Com. v. i. p. 368.

While

While the numbers of our people were thus
augmented from various fources, Edward VI. is
faid to have brought over, in 1549, *many thoufands*
of foreign manufacturers, who greatly improved
our own fabricks of various kinds. Yet, they
were not invited into a country, where the lower
orders were even then very free, or very happy.
The act * *for the punifhment of vagabonds and the
relief of the poor*, recites, " Forafmuch as idlenefs
" and vagabondrie is the mother of all thefts and
" other mifchiefs, and the multitude of people
" given thereto has been always here, within this
" kingdom, very great, and more in number than
" in other regions, to the great impoverifhment of
" the realm." This law therefore enacted, That
if any perfon fhall bring before two juftices any
runagate fervant, or any other which liveth idly
and loiteringly by the fpace of three days, the fame
juftices fhall caufe the faid idle and loitering fervant or vagabund to be marked on the breaft
with the mark of V by a hot iron, and fhall ad-
judge him to be a *flave* to the perfon who brought
him, and who may caufe him to work, by beating,
chaining, or otherwife. The unenlightened makers
of this difgraceful effort of legiflation became
foon fo afhamed, as to repeal the law, which they
ought to have never made. And were it not, that
it fhews the condition of the country, and the
modes of thinking of the higher orders, in 1547,

* 1 Edward VI. ch. 3.

it

it might, without much lofs, be expunged from
the ftatute book.

But the legiflators of this reign were more happy in fome other of their laws. They reftored the
ftatute of treafons of Edward III.; they encouraged the fifheries to Iceland, to Newfoundland,
and to Ireland. They inflicted penalties on the
follers of victuals, who were not content with reafonable profit, and on artificers and labourers, con-
fpiring the time and manner of their work. As
" *great inconveniencies, not meet to be rehearfed, had*
" *followed of compelled chaſtity,*" all pofitive laws
againſt the marriage of priefts were repealed.
Manufactures were encouraged, partly by procuring the materials at the cheapeſt rate, but ſtill
more by preventing frauds. And agriculture was
promoted by means of inclofing, which is faid to
have given rife to Ket's rebellion in 1549. This
event alone fufficiently proves, that the people had
confiderably increafed, but had not yet applied ſtea-
dily to labour.

While the abfurd practice continued, during the
reign of Mary, of promoting manufactures by
monopoly, inftead of competition, one law alone
appears to have been attended with effects, continual and falutary. It is the act * " for the mend-
" ing of highways;" being now, fays the law,
" both very noifome and tedious to travel in, and
" dangerous to paffengers and carriages." The

---

* 2 & 3 Philip and Mary, ch. 8.

firſt

firſt effort of Engliſh legiſlation, on a ſubject ſo much
connected with the proſperity of every people, is
the act of Edward I. for enlarging the breadth of
highways from one market town to another. This
law, which was enacted in 1285, was however intended rather to prevent robbery, than to promote
facility in travelling. The roads of particular
diſtricts were amended by ſeveral laws of Henry
VIII. But this of Philip and Mary is the firſt general law, which obliged every pariſh, by four days
labour of its people, to repair its own roads. The
reign of Charles II. merits the praiſe of having
firſt eſtabliſhed turnpikes ; whereby thoſe, who enjoy the benefits of eaſy conveyance, contribute
the neceſſary expence.

Before the commencement of the celebrated
reign of Elizabeth, a conſiderable change had
doubtleſs taken place in our policy, and in the
numbers of our people. Agriculture, manufactures, fiſheries, commerce, diſtant voyages, had
all been begun, and made ſome progreſs, from
the ſpirit that had already been incited. And all
theſe muſt aſſuredly have flouriſhed, during the domeſtic tranquillity of a ſteady government, through
half a century, as well as afterwards, from the
example of œconomy and prudence, of activity
and vigour, which Elizabeth, on all occaſions, ſet
before her ſubjects.

The act of Elizabeth *, containing orders for
artificers, labourers, ſervants of huſbandry, and ap-

* 5 Eliz. ch. 4.

prentices,

prentices, merits confideration; becaufe we may learn from it the ftate of the country. *Villains*, we fee, from this enumeration, had ceafed, before 1562, to be objects of legiflation. And we may perceive from the recital, " That the wages and " allowances, rated in former ftatutes, are in divers " places too fmall, and *not anfwerable to this time,* " refpecting *the advancement of all things,* belonging " to the faid fervants and labourers,"—a favourable change had taken place in the fortunes of this numerous clafs. This law, particularly where it requires apprenticefhips, ought to be repealed; becaufe its tendency is to abridge the liberty of the fubject, and to prevent competition among workmen.

The fame obfervation may be applied to the act " againft the erecting of cottages *." If we may credit the affertion of the legiflature, " great " multitudes of cottages were daily more and more " increafing, in many parts of this realm." This ftatement evinces an augmentation of people: yet, the execution of fuch regulations, as this law contains, by no means promotes the ufeful race of hufbandry fervants.

The principle of the poor laws, which may be faid to have originated in this reign, as far as it neceffarily confines the labourer to the place of his birth, is at once deftructive of freedom, and of the true interefts of a manufacturing community, that can alone be effectually promoted by competition;

* 13 Eliz. ch. 7.

which

which hinders the rife of wages among workmen, and promotes at once the goodnefs and cheapnefs of the manufacture.

A few falutary laws were doubtlefs made during the reign of Elizabeth. But her legiflation will be found not to merit generally much praife. Her acts for encouraging manufactures by monopoly; for promoting trade by prohibition; and for aiding hufbandry, by preventing the export of corn, alone juftify this remark. Her regulations, for punifhing the frauds, which arife commonly in manufactures when they are encouraged by monopoly, merit commendation.

Having thus fhewn the commencement of an increafing population, amidft famines and war, and traced a confiderable progrefs, during ages of healthfulnefs and quiet, it is now time to afcertain the precife numbers, which probably exifted in England, towards the end of Queen Elizabeth's reign.

From the documents, which ftill remain in the *Mufeum*, it is certainly known, that very accurate accounts were often taken of the people, by the intelligent minifters of that great princefs. Harrifon, who has tranfmitted an elaborate defcription of England, gives us the refult of the mufters of 1575, when the number of fighting men was found to be   —   1,172,674: Adding withal, that it was believed a full third had been omitted. Notwithftanding the greatnefs of this number, fays Mr. Hume, the fame author *complains much of the decay of populoufnefs*; a vulgar

D   complaint

complaint in all ages and places*. Sir Walter
Raleigh however afferts, that there was a general
review, in 1583, of all the men in England, ca-
pable of bearing arms, who were found to amount
to — — 1,172,000

Here then are two credible evidences to an important fact : That, in 1575, or 1583, the fighting
men of England, according to enumerations,
amounted to — — 1,172,000
Which, if multiplied by 4, would prove
the men, women, and children to
have been — 4,688,000

Without comparing minutely the numbers, which
we have already found, in 1377, with the people,
who thus plainly exifted in 1577, it is apparent,
that there had been a vaft increafe in the intermediate two hundred years. Such then were the

---

* Hift. vol. v. p. 481. — vi. p. 179. By endeavouring to collect every thing that could throw light on the population of Elizabeth's reign, Mr. Hume has bewildered himfelf and his reader. Peck has preferved a paper, which, by proving that there
were mufters in 1575, confirms Harrifon's account. [Defid.
Curiofa, v. i. p. 74.] It is a known fact, that there was an
enumeration of the mariners, in 1582, which correfponds with
Raleigh's account. [Campbel's Pol. Survey, v. i. p. 161.]
That there were feveral feveral furveys then, is a fact incontrovertible ; as appears indeed from the Harl. MSS. in Brit.
Muf. Nos. 412 and 6,839. The Privy Council having required the Bifhops, in July 1563, to certify the number of *families* in their feveral diocefes, were informed minutely of
the particulars of each. Some of the Bifhops returns may be
feen in MSS. Harl. No. 595. Brit. Muf. From the Bifhops certificates, as well as from the 31 Eliz. ch. 7. it appears, that the words *families* and *houfeholds* were then ufed
fynonymoufly.

numbers

numbers of the fighting men, and of the inhabitants of England, during the reign of Elizabeth: and fuch was the power, wherewith that illuftrious Queen defended the independence of the nation, and fpread wide its renown.[*].

But, it is the ardour with which a people are infpired, more than their numbers, that conftitutes their real force. It was the enmity wherewith *the armada* had infpired England againft Spain, which prompted the Englifh people, rather than the Englifh court, to aid the baftard Don Antonio to conquer Portugal : and *twenty thoufand* volunteers engaged in this romantic enterprize, under thofe famous leaders Norris and Drake.—An effort, which fhewed the manners of the age more than its populoufnefs, ended in difappointment, as

[*] The particular number of the *communicants* and *recufants*, in each diocefe and parifh of England, was certified to the Privy Council, by the Bifhops, in 1603.—MSS: Harl. Brit. Muf. No. 280.

And the number of communicants was - 2,057,033
Of recufants - - - - 8,465
                                    ──────────
In all - 2,065,498

By the 33d Eliz. chap. 1. all perfons upwards of fixteen years of age were required to go to church, under the penalty of twenty pounds. If the 2,065,498 contained all the perfons, both male and female, who were thus required to frequent the church, this number would correfpond very well with the fighting men lately ftated; and fhew the people of England and Wales to have been between four and five millions, during Elizabeth's reign, though approaching nearer to the laft number than the firft.

might

might have been forefeen, if enthufiafm and reafon were not always at variance. An alarm being given of an invafion by the Spaniards, in
1599, the Queen equipped a fleet, and levied an
army, in a fortnight, to oppofe them. Nothing,
we are told, gave foreigners a higher idea of the
power of England than this fudden armament.
Yet, it is not too much to affert, that Lancafhire
alone, confidering its numerous manufactories and
extenfive commerce, is now able to make a more
fteady exertion*, amidft modern warfare, than the
whole kingdom in the time of Elizabeth.

The acceffion of James I. was an event aufpi-
cious to the profperity and the populoufnefs of
Great Britain. The tranquillity of the Northern
counties of England, which it had been the object of fo many of Elizabeth's laws to fettle, was

* The traders of Liverpool alone fitted out, at the commencement of the late war with France, between the 26th of
August 1778 and the 17th of April 1779, a hundred and twenty privateers, armed each with ten to thirty guns, but moftly
with fourteen to twenty. From an accurate lift, containing
the name and appointment of each, it appears, that thefe
privateers meafured 30,787 tons, carrying 1,986 guns, and
8,754 men. The fleet fent againft the armada, in 1588,
meafured 31,985 tons, and was navigated by 15,272 feamen.
And, from the efforts of a fingle town we may infer, that the
private fhips of war formed a greater force, during the war of
the Colonies, than the nation, with all its unanimity and zeal,
was able to equip under the potent government of Elizabeth.
There was an enumeration, in 1581, of the fhipping and failors of England, which amounted to 72,450 tons, and
14,295 mariners. To this ftatement, Doctor Campbel adds,
That the feamen of the fhips regiftered in the port of London, in 1732, were 21,797. [Pol. Survey, vol. i. p. 161.]

.2   at

at once reſtored : and the two-and-twenty years
of uninterrupted peace, during the preſent reign,
muſt have produced the moſt ſalutary effect on
the induſtry of the people, though this circumſtance has caſt an unmerited ridicule on the
King.

The various laws which were paſſed by this
monarch, for ſuppreſſing the frauds of manufacturers, evince at once, that they had increaſed in
conſiderable numbers, and muſt have continued
to increaſe. The acts for reformation of ale-
houſes, and repreſſing of drunkenneſs, as they
plainly proceeded from the puritaniſm of the times,
muſt have promoted ſobriety of manners, and attention to buſineſs. The act for the relief and
regulation of perſons infected with the plague
muſt have had its effect, in preventing the frequent return of this deſtructive evil. Domeſtic
induſtry was doubtleſs promoted by the act againſt
monopolies : and foreign commerce was aſſuredly
extended by the law, enabling all perſons to trade
with Spain, Portugal, and France. But, above
all, the agricultural intereſts of the nation were
enſured by the act for confirming the poſſeſſion
of copyholders ; and ſtill more, by the law for the
general quiet of the ſubject, againſt all pretences
of dormant claims on the lands, which had de-
ſcended from remote anceſtors to the then poſſeſ-
ſors. Of this ſalutary law the principle was adopted,
and its efficacy enforced, by a legiſlative act of the
preſent reign.

A com-

A comparifon of the laws, which were enacted by the parliaments of Elizabeth and of James, would leave a decided preference to the parliamentary leaders of the laft period, both in wifdom and in patriotifm. The private acts of parliament, in Elizabeth's time, were made chiefly to *reftore the blood* of thofe, who had been attainted by her predeceffors: the private acts of James were almoft all made for *naturalizing foreigners.* One of the laft parliamentary grants of this reign was £.18,000 for the reparation of decaying cities and towns, though it is not now eafy to tell how the money was actually applied.

Elizabeth had begun the practice of giving bounties to the builders of fuch fhips as carried *one hundred* tons. James I. merits the praife of giving large fums for the encouragement of this moft important manufacture. And while Charles I. patronized every ornamental art, he gave from a very fcanty revenue a bounty of five fhillings the ton for every veffel of the burthen of *two* hundred tons. Thefe notices enable us to trace the fize of our merchant-fhips through a very active century of years. The minifters of Elizabeth had confidered a veffel of one hundred tons as fufficient for the purpofes of an inconfiderable commerce: the advifers of Charles I. were not fatisfied with fo fmall a fize. It was to this wife policy, that the trading fhips of England were employed, ere long, in protecting her rights, and even in extending her glory.

The

The act which, in 1623, reduced the interest of money to eight *per cent.* from ten, shews sufficiently, even against the preamble, that complains of decline, how much the nation had prospered, and was then advancing to a higher state of improvement. Such laws can never be safely enacted till all parties, the lenders as well as the borrowers, are properly prepared to receive them. The chearfulness of honest Stowe led him to see, and to represent, the state of England, during the reign of James, as it really was. He says, as Camden had said before him in 1580, that it would in time be incredible, were there not due mention made of it, what great increase there is, within these few years, of commerce and wealth throughout the kingdom ; of the great building of royal and mercantile ships ; of the repeopling of cities, towns, and villages ; beside the sudden augmentation of fair and costly buildings. The great measure of the present reign, which was productive of effects, lasting and unhappy, was the settlement of colonies beyond the Atlantic.

Lord Clarendon exhibits a picture equally flattering, of the condition of England, during the peaceful years of Charles I. And the representation of this great historian is altogether consistent with probability and experience. The vigorous spirit, which Elizabeth had bequeathed to her people, continued to operate, long after she had ceased to delight them by her presence, or to protect them by her wisdom. The laws of former legislators produced successively their tardy effects. And it

ought

ought to be remembered, that neither difputes among the great, parliamentary altercations, nor even civil contefts, till they proceed the length of tumult and bloodfhed, ever produce any bad confequences to the induftry, or comfort of the governed.

The civil wars, which began in 1640, unhappy as they were while they continued, both to king and people, produced in the end the moft falutary influences, by bringing the higher and lower ranks clofer together, and by continuing, in all a vigour of defign, and activity of practice, that in prior ages had no example.

One of the firft confequences of real hoftilities was the eftablifhment of taxes, to which the people had feldom contributed, and which produced, before the conclufion of warfare, the enormous fum of £. 95,512,095 *. The gallant fupporters of Charles I. gave the fovereign, whom they loved amidft his diftreffes, large fums of money, while confifcations left them any thing to give. Here then, were the mines of Potofi opened in England. The opulence, which induftry had been collecting for ages, was now brought into action, by the arts of the tax-gatherer: and the country-gentlemen, who had long complained *of a fearcity of money*, contributed greatly, by unlocking their

---

* Stevens's Hift. of Taxes, p. 296. But Stevens includes the fales of confifcated lands, compofitions for eftates, and fuch other more oppreffive modes of raifing money. There were collected, by *excifes* only, £. 10,200,000 ; and by tonage and poundage £. 5,700,000.

coffers, to remove the evil, that they had themfelves created by hoarding.

One of the firft effects of civil commotion was
the placing of private money in the fhops of gold-
fmiths, for its better fecurity, and for the advantage of the intereft, which, at the commencement
of banking, was allowed the proprietors. By facilitating the ready transfer of property, and the
eafy payment of private debts, as well as public
impofts, *banking* may be regarded as the fruitful
mother of *circulation*. The collecting of taxes,
and the fubfequent expenditure, raifed ere long
the price of all things. Owing to thofe caufes
chiefly, the legal intereft of money was reduced,
in 1651, to fix *per cent*. And the reduction of
intereft is at once a proof of previous acquifition,
and a means of future profperity.

The Reftoration of Charles II. induced the people to transfer the energy, which they had exerted
during twenty years hoftilities, to the various operations of peace. The feveral manufactories, and
new productions of hufbandry, that were introduced from foreign countries, before *the Revolution* formed a new epoch, alone evince a vigorous
application to the ufeful arts, in the intermediate
period. The common highways were enlarged
and repaired, while turnpikes were placed on the
great Northern road, in the counties of Hertford, Huntingdon, and Cambridge. Rivers were
deepened for the purpofes of internal conveyance
by water. The acts of navigation created fhip-
carpenters and failors. Foreign trade was increafed

creafed by opening new markets, and by withdraw-
ing the alien duties, which had always obftructed
the vent of native manufactures. Thofe meafures
alone, that at once made internal communications
eafy and fafe, would have promoted the profperity and population of any country.

But, above all, the change of manners, and the
intermixture of the higher and middle ranks, by
marriages, induced the gentry, and even the
younger branches of the nobility, to bind their
fons apprentices to merchants, and thereby to eno-
ble a profeffion, that was before only gainful; to
invigorate traffic by their greater capitals, and to
extend its operations by their fuperior knowledge.
Hence Child, Petty, and Davenant agreed in afferting *, in oppofition to the party writers of the
times, that the commerce and riches of England
did never, in any former age, encreafe fo faft as in
the bufy period from the Reftoration to the Revolution.

From the foregoing circumftances we may infer a confiderable augmentation of inhabitants,
the more important to the ftate, becaufe they were

* The Board of Trade reprefented in December 1697:
"We have made inquiry into the ftate of trade in general,
"from the year 1670 to the prefent time: and from the beft
"calculations we can make, by the duties paid at the Cuftom-
"houfe, we are of opinion, that trade in general did confi-
"derably increafe, from the end of the Dutch war in 1673, to
"1689, when the late war began." Yet, the Board feem not
to have attended to the 25 Cha. II. ch. 6; which wifely
enacted, That Denizens and Aliens fhould pay no more taxes
for the native commodities of this kingdom, or for fifh caught
in Englifh fhips, when exported, than fubjects.

the

the moft induftrious. But many emigrated, it has
been faid, to the colonies, and many perifhed by
peftilence. Yet, the Lord Chief Juftice Hale infifts, " That mankind hath ftill increafed, even to
" manifeft fenfe and experience:" and becaufe,
fays he, this is an affertion of fact, it is impoffible
to be made out, but by inftances of fact. If however, he adds, we fhould inftitute a comparifon between the prefent time (1670), and the beginning
of Queen Elizabeth's reign (1558), and compare
the number of trained foldiers then and now, the
number of fubfidy men then and now, they will
eafily give an account of a very great increafe of
people within this kingdom, even to admiration *.

A mere queftion of fact, with regard to the
ber of births at any two diftant periods, may
be either confirmed, or difproved, by an

---

* See Lord Hale's convincing argument, in *The Origination
of Mankind confidered*, ch. 10. Sir John Dalrymple found, in
King William's cabinet, a minute account of the number of
freeholders in England, which was taken by order of that monarch, in order to find out the proportion between church-
men, diffenters, and papifts; and which Sir John has publifhed in the Appendix to his Memoirs:

	Conformifts.	Non Con.	Papifts.
In Canterbury and York -	2,477,254	108,676	13,856
Contraft with thefe the be-			
fore-mentioned commu-			
nicants and recufants, in			
1603 — —	2,057,033	—	8,465

This comparifon, after allowing for the original inaccura-
cies of both accounts, fhews a great change in the numbers, in
the opinions, and practice of the people, from 1603 to 1689.

appeal

appeal to the parish registers; which, containing a collection of facts, may be regarded as one of the best proofs, that the nature of the enquiry admits. And the Lord Chief Justice Hale remarked of them, because he was struck with the force of their evidence, *That they give a greater demonstration of the gradual increase of mankind, than a hundred notional arguments can either evince or confute.* For, a greater number of births, in any one period more than in any other, must proceed from a greater number of breeders; which evinces a more numerous population. And from an attentive examination of such proofs, Graunt proceeded*, in 1662, to shew, with greater ability, the progressive increase of the people, and to prove how easily the country could supply the capital with numerous recruits, without any sensible diminution.

Having thus traced a gradual progress in population, it is now time to ascertain the precise numbers at the Revolution. And Gregory King, who has been praised by Davenant for his research and his skilfulness, has left us documents, from which we may form an estimate sufficiently accurate. From an inspection of the hearth books, and the

---

* See The Observations on the Bills of Mortality. Doctor Price has quoted Tindal, for the fact, That there appeared, by the hearth books of 1665, in England and Wales,

$$1,230,000 \text{ houses.}$$

The acknowledged number in 1690 — 1,300,000

This, if we may credit Tindal, is sufficient evidence of a rapid increase in no long period. Graunt calculated the people of England and Wales, in 1662, at 6,440,000 persons.

assessments

aſſeſſments on marriages, births, and burials, King formed calculations of the numbers of families, houſes, and people ; which, according to Davenant, " were perhaps more to be relied upon, than " any thing that had been ever done of the like " kind."

It had been the faſhion of the preceding age to ſtate the numbers of mankind in every country too high : from this period ingenious men were carried away by a reprehenſible ſelf-ſufficiency to calculate them too low. Of the ſtatements of King, it was remarked by Sir Robert Harley [*], in 1697, " Theſe aſſeſſments are no good foundation ; heads " at a medium being (according to the computa- " tion) *per* houſe in London only *five*: omiſſions " in the country are probably greater than in Lon- " don, becauſe numbering the people is there more " terrible. The polls are inſtances: families of " ſeven or eight perſons, being not numbered at " above three or four perſons in ſome remote " counties." Yet, by thus calculating $4\frac{1}{17}$, inſtead of 5, in every *family*; which was ſtill conſidered as ſynonymous with *houſehold*, this would demonſtrate an increaſe of a million, during the foregoing century.

Davenant, by publiſhing only extracts from King's obſervations, and by ſpeaking confuſedly of *families* and *houſes*, has done an injury to King, and to truth. All will appear conſiſtent and clear,

[*] Harl. MSS. in the Muſeum, Nos. 6,837—7,021.

when

when this ingenious calculator is allowed to speak
for himself.

The number of *houses* in the kingdom, as
charged, says he, in the books of the Hearth Office
at Lady Day 1690, were, — 1,319,215:
But, whereas the chimney money being charged on
the tenant, or inhabitant, the divided houses stand as
so many distinct dwellings, in the accounts of the
said Hearth Office. And whereas the empty houses,
smith's shops, &c. are included in the said account, all which may very well amount to 1 in
36 or 37, (or near 3 *per cent.*) which, in the whole,
may be about 36,000 houses; it follows, that the
true number of *inhabited houses* is not above

1,290,000;

which, however, we shall call, in round

numbers, — — 1,300,000

Having thus adjusted the number of houses, we
come now, continues he, to apportion the number
of souls to each, according to what we have observed from the said assessments on marriages,
births, and burials.

London

London within the walls produced
almoſt - - - 5¼ *per* houſe.
Sixteen pariſhes without, full - 4¼
The reſt of the bills of mortality al-
moſt - - - 4¼
The other cities and market towns 4¼
The villages and hamlets - 4

So, London and
the bills of mortality contained - -

	Inhabited houſes.	*per* houſe.	Souls.
So, London and the bills of mortality contained	105,000	at 4,57	479,600
The cities and market towns	195,000	4,3	838,500
The villages and hamlets	1,000,000	4	4,000,000
In all	1,300,000	4,9	5,318,100

But, conſidering that the omiſſions in the ſaid
aſſeſſments may well be,
In London and the
bills of morta-
lity - - - - 10 *per cent.* or 47,960 ſouls
In the cities and
market towns - 2 *per cent.* or 16,500
In the villages and
hamlets - - 1 *per cent.* or 40,000

In all - - - 104,460 ſouls:

It

It follows, that the true number of people, dwelling in the 1,300,000 *inhabited houses*, should be - - - 5,422,560.

Lastly; whereas the number of transitory people, as seamen and soldiers, may be accounted 140,000; whereof nearly one half, or 60,000, have no place in the said assessments: and that the number of vagrants, as hawkers, pedlars, crate carriers, gipsies, thieves, and beggars, may be reckoned 30,000; whereof above one half, or 20,000, may not be taken notice of in the said assessments, making in all 80,000 persons: It follows, that the whole number of people in England and Wales is much about 5,500,000, viz.

In London - - 530,000 souls
In the other cities and towns - 870,000
In the villages and hamlets - 4,100,000

In all - - - 5,500,000

The number of inhabited *houses*
being about - - 1,300,000
The number of *families* about 1,360,000

The people answer at 4¼ *per* house, and 4 *per* family.

Thus much from **Gregory King's** Political Observations [*]. And his statements are doubtless very curious, and even exact, though we now know,

[*] There is a very fair copy of King's Obfervations, in MSS. Harl. Brit. Muf. No. 1,898.

that

that the number of dwellers, which he allowed to every houfe, and to every family, was a good deal under the truth, as Sir Robert Harley at the time fufpected.

Subfequent inquirers have enumerated the houfes and the inhabitants of various villages, towns, and cities, inftead of relying on the defective returns of tax-gatherers. Doctor Price is now difpofed to admit, from the enumerations which he had feen, that *five perfons and a fixth*, refide in every houfe[*]. Mr. Howlet, from a ftill greater number of enumerations, infifts [†] for five and two-fifths. It will at laft be found, perhaps [‡], that five and two-fifths are the

---

[*] Reverfionary Payments, v. ii. p. 288.

[†] Examination of Price, p. 145.

[‡] In 1773, Dr. Price infifted, that there were *not quite five in every houfe*. [Obfervations on Reverfionary Payments, 3d edition, p. 184.] In 1783, the Doctor feemed willing to allow five one-fixth in every houfe: But he ftill contends, That if you throw out of the calculation Liverpool, Manchefter, Birmingham, and other populous towns, the number in every houfe *ought to be lefs than five*. [Obfervations on Reverfionary Payments, 4th edit, v. ii. p. 288—9.] The Rev. Mr. New made a very accurate enumeration of the parifh of St. Philip and St. Jacob in the city of Briftol, during the year 1781, and found 1,529 inhabited houfes, and therein 9,850 fouls. Thefe numbers prove, that more than fix one-third dwell in every houfe. And from this enumeration we may infer, That in the full inhabited city of Briftol, fix at leaft refide in every houfe. If, in the fpirit of Doctor Price, we throw out of the calculation all populous places, and ftudioufly collect fuch decaying towns as Sandwich, the proportion to every houfe muft be limited to *five*.

E.   fmalleft

smalleſt number, which, on an average of the whole kingdom, dwells in every houſe.

Little doubt can ſurely now remain of there having been in England and Wales 1,300,000 inhabited houſes at the Revolution. Were we to multiply this number by *five*, it would demonſtrate a population of ſix millions and a half: were we to multiply by five and two-fifths, or even by five and one-fifth, this operation would carry the number up nearly to ſeven millions: and ſeven millions were conſidered, by ſome of the moſt intelligent men of that day, as the people of this kingdom at the Revolution.

But, if we take the loweſt number, of ſix millions and a half, and compare it with five millions, the higheſt number aſſuredly in 1588, this compariſon would evince an increaſe of a million and a half in the ſubſequent century, and nearly four millions and a half from 1377. Yet, Doctor Price regards the epoch of the *Reformation* (1517) as a period of greater population than the preſent.

In giving an account of the reign of King William, Sir John Dalrymple remarks, That *three and twenty regiments were compleated in ſix weeks.* This is doubtleſs an adequate proof of the ardour of the times, but it is a very ſlight evidence of an overflowing populouſneſs. Want of employment often ſends recruits to an army, which, in more induſtrious years, would languiſh without hope of reinforcements. We may learn, indeed, from Sir Joſiah Child, That it was a queſtion agitated, during

ing

ing the reign of Charles II. "If we have more
"people now than in former ages, how came it to
"pass, that in the times of Henry IV. and V. and
"even in prior times, we could raise such great ar-
"mies, and employ them in foreign wars, and
"yet retain a sufficient number to defend the
"kingdom, and to cultivate our lands at home?
"I answer first," says this judicious writer, "that
"bigness of armies is not a certain indication of
"the numerousness of a nation, but sometimes of
"the government and distribution of the lands;
"where the prince and lords are owners of the
"whole territory: although the people be thin,
"the armies upon occasion may be very great, as
"in Fez and Morocco. Secondly, princes ar-
"mies in Europe are become more proportion-
"able to their purses, than to the numbers of their
"people.

Thus much it was thought proper to premise,
with regard to the previous condition and policy of
England, as well as its anterior populousness to
The Revolution, when THIS ESTIMATE begins.

THEORISTS are not agreed, in respect to
those circumstances, which form the strength of nations, either actual or comparative. One considers
the power of a people " to consist in their numbers and wealth." Another insists, " that the
force of every community most essentially depends

on

on the capacity, valour, and union of the lead-
ing characters of the state." And a third, adopting partly the sentiments of both, contends, " that
though numbers and riches are highly important,
and the resources of war may decide a contest
where other advantages are equal; yet the resources of war, in hands that cannot employ them,
are of little avail, since manners are as essential
as either people or wealth."

It is not the purpose of this Estimate to amuse
the fancy with uninstructive definitions, or to be-
wilder the judgment with verbal disputations, as
unmeaning as they are unprofitable. The glories
of the war of 1755 have cast a continued ridicule
on the far-famed *Estimator of the manners and principles of the times.* Recent struggles have thrown
equal ridicule on other calculators of an analogous
spirit. And we may find reason in the end to
conclude, that the qualities of the mind, either
vigorous or effeminate, have undergone no unhappy change, whatever alteration there certainly
is in the labour of the hands of our people, from
the epoch of the Revolution to the present moment.

But from general remark, let us descend to minute investigations, with regard to the progressive
numbers of the people, to the extent of their industry, and to the successive amount of their traffic and accumulations; because our resources arose
then, as they arise now, *from the land and labour
of this island alone.*

The

The infult offered by France to the fovereignty
of England, by giving an afylum to an abdicated
monarch, and by difputing the right of a high-
minded people to regulate their own affairs, forced
King William into an eight years war with that
potent country, which he perfonally hated, and with
which he ardently wifhed to quarrel. He had
therefore no inclination to weigh in very fcrupulous fcales the wealth of his fubjects againft the
greater opulence of their rivals, who were in thofe
days more induftrious, and were further advanced
in the practice of manufacture, and knowledge of
traffic. Yet the defire of that warlike monarch
being feconded by the zeal of a people, whofe refources were not then equal to their bravery, he was
enabled to engage in an arduous difpute for the
moft honourable end. Happy! had hoftilities ended,
as foon as the independence of the nation was vin-
dicated from infult.

We may form a fufficient judgment of the
ftrength of England at that æra from the following detail :

The number of *fighting men*, according to the
calculation of Gregory King, as cited with appro-
bation by Davenant, was 1,308,000 ; yet the one
fourth of the people formed the men fit for war,
whatever may have been the real population of
England, during the reign of King Williar.

E 3   The

The yearly income of the nation from its land and labour amounted, if we may credit the ftatement of King, to - - - £.43,500,000

The yearly expence of the people for their neceffary fubfiftence - - 41,700,000

The yearly accumulation of profit £. 1,800,000

The value of the whole kingdom, according to King, £.650,000,000 * ; which, forming the capital whence income arofe, was no proper fund for taxation.

Davenant ftates, from various *conjectures* and *calculations*, the circulating money at £.18,500,000 †, while there yet exifted in the nation no paper-money, and little circulation ; which, by facilitating the eafy transfer of property, is fo favourable to the levying of taxes.

* See King's Polit. Obferv. in MSS. Harl. Brit. Muf. No. 1,898.

† Gregory King having ftated the filver coin at eight million and a half in 1688, and the gold coin at three million, Sir Robert Harley thereupon remarked, " That the mint accounts would make us believe there is more gold coin than three million ; but both accounts together would make a good eftimate."—MSS. Harl. Brit. Muf. 1,898. The circulating *coin* may therefore be taken at eleven million and a half during King William's reign. It is one of the tenets of Doctor Price, to maintain, that we had more coins in circulation, during thofe times than at prefent.

King

King James's annual income amounted only to
£.2,061,856. 7s. 9 ¼d.*; which is a greater revenue than any of his predeceffors had ever enjoyed.

Of. this there remained in the exchequer, on
the 5th of November, 1688, £.80,138 †; which
little enabled King William either to defray the
expences of the Revolution, or to prepare for
war.

The nett income paid into the exchequer, in
1691, from the cuftoms and excife, from the land,
and from polls, amounted only to £.4,249,757;
of which there were applied towards carrying on
the war £.3,393,634; and to the fupport of the
government £.856,123 ‡.

The average of the annual fupplies, during the
war, which were raifed with difficulty from a diffatisfied people, amounted only to £.5,105,505 §;
whence we may form an opinion of the force
which could then be exerted, though it muft be
admitted, that the fame nominal fum had in thofe
days a greater power.

---

* Hift. of Debts, p. 6—7.

† For the accurate informations, which thefe fheets convey
from a tranfcript of the Exchequer-books in King William
and Queen Anne's reigns, the public owe an additional ob-
ligation, and the compiler a kindnefs, to the liberal commu-
nication of Mr. Aftle.

‡ Mr. Aftle's Tranfcript.　　　　§ Id.

There were borrowed by the government, at an
interest of seven and eight *per cent.* while the
legal interest of money was only six, from
the 5th of November, 1688, to Lady-day,
1702 - - - - £.44,100,795 ;
Of which there were mean while
repaid - - - 34,034,018 ;
Of this debt there remained due at
Lady-day, 1702 * - £.10,066,777

So unfruitful had each branch of taxes proved,
during every year of the war, that the revenue, which had existed before it began, fell
above one half in five years † ; and the deficiencies appeared to have swelled, before the sef-
fion of 1696, to the then enormous sum of
£.6,000,460 ; which greatly enfeebled every exertion of the government, by the advance in the
price of all things. The annual collection of
taxes, to the amount of two million and a half,
more than had been levied on the country in preceding times, while their foreign trade was cut off,
was alone sufficient to embarrass a people of greater
powers of industry and circulation. It is an instructive fact, which is transmitted by Davenant,
that imposts did not then enhance the price of the
commodity to the consumer, when in its highest

* Mr. Astle's Transcript. † Davenant's Essay on
Ways and Means

state

ftate of improvement, but fell on the grower,
who fold the article in its rudeft condition: the
excife did not raife the price of malt, but lowered
the price of barley. And this evinces how much
confumption was embarraffed, and circulation obftructed, during the diftreffes of the Revolution
war.

The annual value of the furplus produce of the
land and labour of England, which was then exported to foreign countries, amounted only to
£.4,086,087. Had the coins of England been
as numerous as Davenant fuppofes them, they
could not long have carried on a war beyond the
limits of the empire. And the cargoes, which
were thus fent abroad, could not, from their inconfiderablenefs, have filled a mighty void for any
length of years.

The tonnage of Englifh fhipping, which were
annually employed for the exportation of the be--
fore-mentioned cargoes, amounted only to 190,533
tons; which, if we allow them to have been navigated at the rate of twelve mariners to every two
hundred tons, required only 11,432 failors; yet
this was the principal nurfery, whence the navy
of England could alone be manned, during the
wars of King William.

The

The following statement will give us ideas sufficiently accurate of the progressive force of the
royal fleet;

	Tons.		Sailors.
Which in 1660 carried	62,594	-	—
In 1675 -	69,681	-	30,951
In 1688 -	101,032	-	—
In 1695 -	112,400	-	45,000

Such, then, was the naval force that, during
the hostilities of William, could be sent into the
line against the potent navy of France, which, in
one busy reign, had been created, and raised to
greatness. It was found almost impossible to man
the fleet, though the admiralty were empowered
by Parliament to lay strict embargoes on the merchants ships *. And this alone ought to give us
a lesson of what importance it is to the state to
augment the native race of carpenters and sailors
by every possible means.

The

---

* Sir J. Dalrymple has published a paper [Appendix,
p. 242.] in order to justify King William from the charge—
" of not exerting the natural strength of England in a sea-
war against France, after the battle of La Hogue ;" which
proves, that his ministers thought it impossible to increase the
fleet ;—" as not having ships enough, nor men, unless we
stop even the craft-trade." There are a variety of documents
in the Plantation-office, which demonstrate the same position.
And see the following comparative view of the fleets of France
and England in 1693.

The great debility of England, during the war of the Revolution, arose from the practice of hoarding in times of diftruft, which prevented circulation; from the diforders of the coin, that only augmented the former evil, while the government iffued tallies of wood for the fupplying of fpecie; from the inability of the people to pay taxes, while they could find no circulating value, either for their labour or property : add to thefe, the turbulence of the lower orders, and the treachery of the great. And above all, if we may believe the minifters of William *, *Nobody knew one day what a Houfe of Commons would do the next.*

It is now time to enquire into the loffes of our trade, during that diftrefsful war. A more con-

---

The following "Comparifon of the French and Englifh fleets in 1693, formed from lifts brought into the Houfe of Commons by Secretary Trenchard," will fhew how nearly equal they were in force, even fubfequent to the victory of La Hogue in the preceding year. [Bibl. Harley, Brit. Mufeum, No. 1,898.]

	French Fleet.			English Fleet.			Difference.	
Ships from	At Breft.	At Toulon.	Total.	In being.	Build-ing.	Total.	More.	Lefs.
40 to 50 guns	3	5	8.	31	0	31.	23	0.
50 to 60	10	4	14.	7	1	8.	0	6.
60 to 70	23	9	32.	14	3	17.	0	15.
70 to 80	13	3	16.	23	2	25.	9	0.
80 to 90	7	1	8.	8	6	14.	6	0.
90 to 100	6	4	10.	11	0	11.	1	0.
100 to 108	6	1	7.	5	0	5.	0	2.
	68	27	95.	99	12	111.	39	23.

* Dal. Mem. Appendix, p. 240.

firmed

(60)

firmed commerce could not have ftood fo rude a
fhock as our manufactures and commerce received,
from the imbecility of friends, no lefs than from
the vigour of foes, amidft a difaftrous courfe of
hoftilities of eight years continuance. And the
clamours, which were in the end raifed againft the
managers of the marine, were affuredly founded in
prodigious loffes. An examination of the following proofs will evince this melancholy truth :

Years.	Ships cleared outwards. Tons Eng.	D° foreign.	Total.	Value of their cargoes. £.
1688 —	190,533 —	95,267 —	285,800 —	4,086,087
1696 —	91,767 —	83,024 —	174,791 —	2,729,520
Annual lofs	98,766 —	12,243 —	111,009 £.	1,356,567

The nett revenue of the pofts in — 1688 £. 76,318
D°. — — 1697 58,672*

Dr. Davenant took a different way to go to the
fame point, becaufe he had not accefs to a better.
Having ftated the yearly amount of the cuftoms,
from 1688 to 1695 inclufive, he inferred from the
annual defalcations : " So that it appears fuffi-
" ciently, that in general, fince this war, our trade
" is very much diminifhed, as by a medium of
" feven years the cuftoms are leffened about
" £. 138,707. 7 s. a year." Dr. Davenant juftly
complained of the breaches of the Act of Navigation, " during the flack adminiftration of this
" war;" fo that ftrangers feem to have beaten us

* Mr. Aftle's Tranfcript.

out

out of our own ports. For it was obferved, that there were, in the port of London,

	Tons English.	Do. foreign.	Total.
During the year 1695*	— 65,788	— 83,238	— 149,026

It would be injurious to conceal, that the fame able author, who feems, however, to have fome-times complained without a caufe, acknowledged, " That perhaps no care nor wifdom in the world " could have fully protected our trade during this " laft war with France."

An attentive examination of the numbers of our fhips cleared outwards, and of the cargoes export-ed in them, will convince every candid mind, that in every war there is a point of depreffion in trade, as there is in all things, beyond which it does not decline; and from which it gradually rifes beyond

---

* If with the year mentioned by Davenant, we contraſt the following years, we fhall fee an aftonifhing increafe of the na-vigation and commerce of London. Thus, there were entered in this great port,

	Tons Englifh.	Dº foreign.	Total.
In 1710 —	70,915	— 40,280	— 110,195
19 —	187,122	— 11,468	— 198,590
58 —	125,086	— 69,060	— 194,146
82 —	210,656	— 125,248	— 335,904
83 —	277,797	— 169,170	— 446,967
84 —	372,775	— 92,043	— 464,818

the

the extent of its former greatneſs, unleſs it meets with additional checks. And the year 1694* marked, probably, the loweſt ſtate to which the

---

* The following detail, from the Plantation-office, will give the reader a ſtill clearer view of the navigation of England, during the embarraſſments of the Revolution war.

	Ships cleared outwards.			Ships entered inwards.		
	Tons English.	Do foreign.	Total.	Tons English.	Do foreign.	Total.
1693 London,	44,912	59,750	104,662	36,512	80,875	117,387
Outports,	73,176	28,752	101,928	32,616	27,876	60,492
Total,	118,088	88,502	208,590	69,128	108,751	177,879
				Balance of Trade,		28,611
						206,590
1694 London,	39,648	41,500	81,148	59,472	76,500	135,972
Outports,	33,408	28,224	61,632	35,158	28,910	64,068
Total,	73,056	69,724	142,780	94,630	105,410	200,040
	Balance of Trade,		57,260			
			20,040			

Of the foregoing detail it ought to be obſerved, that it does not appear in the Plantation-office altogether in this form: the number of ſhips, Engliſh and foreign, entered either in London or the outports, is only ſpecified, and the average tonnage of each thus particularly given: the Engliſh ſhips in the port of London were eſtimated at 112 tons each; the foreign at 125 tons each: the Engliſh ſhips at the outports at 72 each; the foreign at 98 tons each. Whence the editor was enabled, by an eaſy calculation, to lay before the public a more preciſe account of the commerce of England, during the war of the Revolution, than has yet been done.

hoſtilities

hoftilities of William beat down the national traffic. But the commerce of England, fuftained by immenfe capitals, and infpired by a happy fkill and diligence, may be aptly compared to a fpring of mighty powers, which always exerts its force in proportion to the weight of its compreffion; and which never fails to rebound with augmented energy, when the preffure is removed by the return of peace. It is neverthelefs a fact equally true, that however the ceffation of war may give frefh ardour to our induftrious claffes at home, and enable our merchants to export cargoes of unexampled extent; yet, there are never wanting writers, who, during this profperous moment, complain of the decline of our manufactories, and the ruin of our trade... It is propofed to illuftrate both thefe facts, in the following fheets; becaufe, from the illuftration we may derive both intelligence and amufement.

Let us then attend to the following proofs:

	Ships cleared outwards.			Value of cargoes exported.
	Tons Eng.	D° foreign.	Total.	£.
Peace of Ryf- wick, 1697	144,264 -	100,524 -	244,788 -	3,525,907
1699 1700 1701	293,703 -	43,625 -	337,328 -	6,709,881

In addition to this fatisfactory detail, let us confider the revenue of the poft-office, which, fhewing the extent of correfpondence at different periods,

rinds, furnishes no bad proof of the progress of commerce. The net income of the ports, according to an average of the eight years of King William's wars £. 67,282
D⁰. of the four years of subsequent peace 82,319*

Yet, amidst all this prosperity, Polexfen, one of the Board of Trade, published *a discourse*†, in 1697, in order to shew, "That, so great had been the losses of a seven years war, if a great stock be absolutely necessary to carry on a great trade, we may reasonably conclude the stock of this nation is so diminished, it will fall short; and that, without prudence and industry, we shall rather consume what is left, than recover what we have lost." Davenant, the antagonist of Polexfen, stunned every coffee-house at the same time with his declamations on the decay of commerce. "It will be a great matter for "the present," says he ‡, "if we can recover the "ground, our trade has lost during the last war." But we have seen, that we had already gained *superior ground* at the precise moment wherein he, in this manner, lamented our recent losses both of shipping and trade. So different are the deductions of theory from the informations of experience, that temporary interruptions are constantly

* Mr. Astle's Transcript. † Discourse on *Trade,*
Coin, and *Paper Credit.* ‡ Discourse on Trade, 1698.

mistaken

miftaken for fymptoms of habitual decline. And our commercial writers, owing to this caufe, are full of well-meaning falfehood, while they fometimes propagate purpofed deception.

The Revolution may juftly be regarded as an event in our annals, the moft memorable and interefting; becaufe its effects have been the happieft, in refpect to the fecurity, the comfort, and profperity of the people. Yet, it has for fome years been infifted, with a plaufibility, which precludes the charge of intended paradox, that every caufe of depopulation—*a devouring capital, the wafte of wars, the drain of ftanding armies, emigrations to the colonies, the engraffing of farms, the inclofing of commons, the high price of provifions, and unbounded luxury*—all have concurred, fince that fortunate æra, to difpeople the nation; the numbers of which, it is pretended, have decreafed a million and a half, and ftill continue to decreafe.

In oppofition to fuch controvertifts it is not fufficient to argue, That, having traced a gradual advance in population, during fix centuries of political diftraction and domeftic mifery, and proved an addition of almoft five millions to the original ftock, in 1066, notwithftanding wafteful wars, defolating famines, and habitual debility; we ought thence to infer, that the pofition of a *decreafing populoufnefs*, during a period the moft free, and profperous, and happy, can alone be maintained, by the decifive proof of enumerations, or at leaft, by a mode of induction equal to them in

F   the

the weight of its inference. It is propofed, then, to continue a brief review of the principal occurrences in our hiftory, fince the year 1688, that could have either carried on the former progrefs of our population, or have promoted a gradual decline.

The Revolution did not indeed produce fo much any alteration in the forms of the conftitution, as it changed the maxims of adminiftration; which have every where fo great an influence on the condition of the governed. Yet, from thence a new æra is faid * to have commenced, in which the bounds of prerogative and liberty have been better defined, the principles of government more thoroughly examined and underftood, and the rights of the fubject more explicitly guarded by legal provifions, than in any other period of the Englifh hiftory. One article alone, in the Declaration of Rights, was worth, on account of the confolation which it adminiftered to the lower orders, the whole expence of the enfuing war: " That exceffive bail fhall not be required, or exceffive fines be impofed, or cruel and unufual punifhments be inflicted. " Philofophers have juftly remarked, that feverity of chaftifement has as natural a tendency to debafe mankind, as mildnefs to elevate them. It was not fo much from the declaration, *that the levying money without confent of Parliament is unlawful,* that private

* Blackft. Com. vol. i. p. 213.

property

property was fecured, as from the impartial adminiftration of juftice, which has regularly flowed
from the independence of the Judges. Anderfon * did not forget to give " a brief view of the
eftablifhment of that free conftitution, as it did
certainly contribute greatly, in its confequences, to
the advancement of our induftry, manufactures,
commerce, and fhipping, as well as of our riches
and people, notwithftanding feveral expenfive and
bloody wars."

The hearth-money was foon after taken away;
" being a great oppreffion (fay the Parliament)
of the poorer fort, and a badge of flavery upon
the whole." During the fame feffion, the firft
bounty was given on the exportation of corn :
" How much," fays that laborious writer, " this
bounty has contributed to the improvement of
hufbandry, is too obvious to be difputed :" and
accordingly, the year 1699 has been noticed as
the epoch of the laft great dearth of corn in England. A flourifhing agriculture muft have neceffarily promoted populoufnefs in two refpects ; by
offering encouragement to labour ; by furnifhing
a fupply of provifions at once conftant and cheap,
which were both extremely irregular in former
times. The act of toleration, which was at the
fame time paffed, by " giving eafe to fcrupulous
confciences," tended to promote our induftry and
traffic, and confequently the progrefs of popula-

* Chron. Acc. of Com. vol. ii. p. 189—95.

tion :

tion: for, we may learn of Sir Josiah Child how many people had been driven out of England, from the rise of the Puritans in the reign of Elizabeth, to the blessed æra of toleration.

On the other hand, it has been already shewn how much the eight-years war, which grew out of the Revolution, distressed the foreign trade of England. As King William employed chiefly the troops of other nations; as the profligate and the idle principally recruited the army; as humanity now softened the rigours of war; it may be justly doubted, if we lost a greater number by the miseries of the camp, than were acquired by the arrival of refugees, who sought security in England. And of this opinion was Doctor Davenant *, who was no unconcerned spectator of those eventful times. Yet, it is a known fact, that the taxes, which were successively imposed, did not produce in proportion to their augmentations. And if we attribute this unfavourable circumstance to the inability and pressures of the people, more than to the novelty of contributions, to the enmity of many against the new government, and to the disorders of the coin, we ought undoubtedly to infer, that the imposition of additional burdens necessarily stopped the progress of numbers.

Nevertheless, internal traffic flourished in the mean time. In 1689, the manufactures of cop-

* Vol. iii, p. 363.

per and brafs were revived, rather than introduced. The Sword-blade company, which fettled in Yorkfhire, " brought* over foreign workmen," The French refugees improved the fabrics of paper and of filk, efpecially the lute-
ftrings and alamodes ; which were fo much encouraged by Parliament, that the weavers, being
greatly increafed in numbers, as well as in info-
lence, before the year 1697, raifed a tumult in
London againft the wearers of Eaft India manufactures †. .The eftablifhment of the Bank of
England in 1694, by facilitating public and private circulation, produced all the falutary effects,
that were originally foretold, becaufe it has been
conftantly managed with a prudence, integrity,
and caution beyond example. By giving encouragement to fifheries, in 1695, a hardy race muft
have been greatly multiplied ; and by encouraging,
in 1696, the making of linens, fubfiftence was
given to the young and the old.

The conclufion of every lengthened war de-
prives many men of fupport, who are therefore
obliged to re-enter once more into the competitions
of the world. Yet, Doctor Davenant ‡ affured the
Marquis of Normanby, in 1699, " that we really
want people and hands to carry on the woollen and
linen manufactories together." Admitting the

* And. Chron. Acc. of Com. vol. ii. p. 191.
† Id. p. 220. ‡ Effay on Eaft India Trade, p. 46.

F 3 truth

truth of an affertion, of which indeed there is no
reafon to doubt, the obfervation is altogether confiftent with facts and with principles. In lefs than
two years from the peace of Ryfwick, the dif-
banded idlers had been all engaged in the manufactories, which we have feen eftablifhed, and in
the foreign traffic, that has been fhewn to have
flourifhed fo greatly from this epoch to the demife of King William. Now, what does the pofition of Davenant prove, more than that uncommon
demand never fails to produce remarkable fcarcity, till a fufficient fupply has been found? And
Sir Jofiah Child was therefore induced, a hundred
years ago, to lay it down as a maxim; *Such as
our employment is for people, fo many will our people
be.* Were we now to compare the circumftance
mentioned by Sir John Dalrymple, of the raifing
of three-and-twenty regiments in fix weeks, during the year 1689, with the fact ftated by Doctor Davenant, " of the fcarcity of hands" in 1699,
we ought to infer, that an alteration of manners,
owing to whatever caufe, had in the mean time
taken place; and that the lower orders of men had
learned from experience, to prefer the gainful employments of peace to the lefs profitable and more
dangerous adventures of war.

Yet, admitting that the *moral caufes* before-
mentioned had naturally produced an augmentation of numbers, during the reign of William, we
ought here to remark, that the people who chiefly
fhared

fhared in the felicities, or were incommoded by the factions of thofe times, muft have drawn their firft breath prior to the Revolution: the middle-aged, and the old, who enacted the laws, and as minifters or magiftrates carried them into execution, muft have been born, during the diftractions of the civil wars, or amid the contefts of the adminiftration of Charles I.: and the gallant youth, who fought by the fide of that warlike monarch, muft have firft feen the light foon after the Reftoration.

But, it ought here to be ftated, as a circumftance, which may be fuppofed to have checked the progrefs of population, that there had been actually raifed, though with fome difficulty, on nearly feven millions of people, in thirteen years * - - £. 58,698,688. 19s. 8d.:

If we average this fum by the number of years, we fhall gain a pretty exact idea of King William's annual income - - £. 4,415,360:

And if from this we deduct King
James's revenue .. - - 2,061,856;
_____

The balance, of - - - - 2,453,504,
will fhew how much more the people were burdened in the latter, than in the former reign.

It has neverthelefs been fhewn, that manufac-

* Mr. Aftle's Tranfcript.

tures

tures flourifhed in the mean time; that there was a great demand for labour; that the foreign traffic and navigation of England doubled, from the peace of Ryfwick to the acceffion of Queen Anne. For, the re-coinage of the filver mean time produced an exhilarating effect on induftry, in the fame proportion as the debafement of the current coin is always difadvantageous to the lower orders, and difhonourable to the ftate. The revival of public credit, after the peace of Ryfwick, and the rifing of the notes of the Bank of England to par, ftrengthened private confidence, at the fame time that thefe caufes invigorated our manufactures and our trade. And the fpirit of population was ftill more animated by the many acts of naturalization, which were readily paffed, during every feffion, in the reign of William; and which clearly evince, how many induftrious foreigners found fhelter in England, from the perfecution of countries, lefs tolerant and free.

A NEW war, ftill more bloody and glorious than the former, enfued on the acceffion of Queen Anne. All Europe either hated the imperioufnefs, or dreaded at length the power, of Lewis XIV. But it was his " owning and declaring the pretended prince of Wales to be king of England, Scotland, and

and Ireland," which was the avowed caufe of the hoftilities of Great-Britain againft France; though private motives have generally more influence than public pretences. When her treafurer fat down to calculate the coft, he found refources in his own prudence. Her general faw armies and alliances rife out of his own genius for war and negotiation. And both eftimated right, fince a favourable change had gradually taken place in the fpirit, as well as in the abilities of the people.

If we inquire more minutely into the national ftrength, we fhall find, that England and Wales now contained about - - 1,700,000 fighting men. The union with Scotland

added to thefe about - 325,000
So the united kingdom ————
contained - - - 2,025,000

But troops, without funds to carry them to war, with all that foldiers require, are of little avail. And happy is it for this nation, at leaft, that there is a fucceffive rife in the accumulations of our wealth, in the fame manner as we have already feen a continual progrefs in our population; owing to the various means, which individuals conftantly ufe, to meliorate their own condition. There can be little doubt then, though Gregory King fuppofed the ccntrary, that the productive capital and annual gains of the people were greater at the acceffion of Anne, than they had been

during

during the preceding reign *, or in any former
period.

Godolphin and Marlborough had not to contend with the embarrassments of their predecessors.
The disorders of the coin, which had so enfeebled
the late administration, had been perfectly cured by
a re-coinage. The high interest, which had been
given, and the still higher profit, that was made, by
purchasing government-securities, had drawn meanwhile much of the hoarded cash within the circle
of commerce. No less than £. 3,400,000 of ham-
mered money, which had been equally locked up,
were brought into action, according to Davenant,
by the act for suppressing it, in 1697. The Bank
of England now lent its aid, by facilitating loans,
and circulating exchequer bills. And the public
debts and additional taxes filled circulation at present, and gave it activity; as they had equally
produced similar effects, when the Long Parliament opened the coffers of England. Owing to all
these causes, the statesmen of the reign of Anne bor-

* After so expensive a war just ended, says Anderson, it
gave foreigners a high idea of the wealth and grandeur of
England, to see *two millions sterling* subscribed for in *three* days,
(by the new East-India Company in 1698) and there were persons ready to subscribe as much more: For, although since
that time higher proofs have appeared of the great riches of
this nation, because our wealth is very visibly increased ; yet,
till then, there had never been so illustrious an instance of
England's opulence. [Chron. Com. vol. ii. p. 223.]

rowed

rowed money at five per cent. in 1702, and never
gave more than fix during the war; which alone
shews how the condition of this country had happily changed, from the time that seven and eight
per cent. were paid, only a few years before.

The taxes yielded nett into the exchequer, during the year 1701   £. 3,769,375.
Of this inconfiderable revenue the
  current fervices for the navy ab-
  forbed   —   £. 1,046,397
    the land fervice —   425,998
    the ordnance   —   49,940
    the civil lift   —   704,339
                  —————
                 2,226,674

There were applied to the
  payment of the princi-
  pal and intereft of debts 1,411,912
                ————— 3,638,586
Balance remaining unapplied —   130,789

                * £. 3,769,375.

The nett fums paid into the exchequer during the year 1703, from
  the cuftoms, excife, poft-office,
  land, and mifcellaneous duties - £. 5,561,944:

        * Mr. Aftle's Tranfcript.

                        Of

Of this fum there were iffued for carrying on the war - £. 3,665,430
For paying the civil lift 589,981
the intereft of loans 430,307
Balance remaining for
the payment of loans,
and other fervices - 875,126
                    ─────── * £. 5,561,944

The taxes, which were annually levied on the
people, during the prefent reign, may be calculated from the nett fums paid into the exchequer
in the years 1707—8—9—10, amounting yearly
to £. 5,272,758. This gives us an idea fufficiently
precife of the pecuniary powers, which could then
be exerted by Britain. But the military operations of the government were more extenfive than
the annual fupplies of the parliament. So that
before Chriftmas 1711, unfunded debts were contracted to the amount of £. 9,471,325. This
fum was then too large, as it is faid, to be borrowed at any rate. The public creditors agreed
to convert their claims into a capital, at a fpecified intereft, with charges of management. And
here is the origin of the South Sea Company and
South Sea Stock.

The fupplies granted, during the prefent reign,
amounted to - - £. 69,815,457. 11s. 3¼d.

The expences of the war, as they were ftated by
the commiffioners of public accounts, amounted to - - - - - £. 65,853,799. 8s. 7¼d. †

* Mr. Aftle's Tranf. † Camp. Pol. Survey, vol. ii. p. 543.

And

And the national debt fwelled, before the 31ft
December 1714, to - £. 50,644,306. 13s: 6¼d. ;
on which was paid an intereft of * £. 2,811,903.
10s. 5¼d. and whfch were all more than counter-
balanced by the legiflative encouragements, that
were given in this reign to domeftic induftry and
foreign trade.

The furplus produce of our land and labour,
which was yearly exported, had mean time rifen to
£. 6,045,432; which equally evinces, that we had
not yet much to fpare, and confequently no vaft
remittance, which could be annually fent abroad
for carrying on the war.

The tonnage of Englifh fhips, which from
time to time tranfported this cargo, and which at
that epoch formed the principal nurfery for the
royal navy, had increafed to - 273,693 tons ;
which muft have been navigated,
if we allow twelve men to every
two hundred tons, by - - - 16,422 failors.

By an enumeration † of the trading veffels of
England, in January 1701, it appeared, that
  London had - - 84,882 tons,
  The out-ports had 176,340
       ——— 261,222; and
that they were navigated by 16,471 men, and
120 boys, or 16,591 failors.

The inconfiderable difference between the enumerated tonnage and mariners, and the tonnage

* Hift. of Debt, p. 80; which gives a particular ftatement.
† A detail in the Plantation-office.

            and

and mariners cleared at the cuſtom-houſe, only
marks, that ſeveral ſhips had entered more than
once, and that a greater number of men were
then allowed to every veſſel than there are now ;
whence we may infer, that the calculation and
the enumeration prove the accuracy of each
other.

	Tons.	Men.
The royal navy, which in 1695 had carried —	112,000	and 45,000,
had mouldered before 1704 * to — —	104,754	— 41,000

Its real force will, however, more clearly appear from the following detail : †

* An admiralty-liſt of all her Majeſty's ſhips and veſſels in
ſea-pay, at home and abroad, on the 27th of February 1703-4,
with the higheſt complement of men, and the numbers borne,
muſtered, and wanting. [From the Paper-office.]

Number of ſhips.			Rates.
5	— of —	2
40	— — —	3
57	— — —	4
33	— — —	5
16	— — —	6,

beſides fire-ſhips,
bombs, and ſmaller veſſels, all which

	Complement of men.	Borne.	Muſtered.
Contained	46,745 —	39,720 —	30,778
Wanting	— —	7,025 —	15,967

† Philips's State of the Nation, p. 35.

Shi

Ships of the line employ-
ed in — 1702 - 74 in 1707 - 72
1703 - 79 — 1708 - 69
1704 - 74 — 1709 - 67
1705 - 79 — 1710 - 62
1706 - 78 — 1711 - 59

Such then was the ftrength of the nation under
Queen Anne. Let us now enquire into the loffes
of our trade during her glorious, but unproduc-
tive, war.

The effort of the belligerent powers was made
chiefly by land ; and the foreign trade of England feems to have rather languifhed, than to have
been overpowered, as it had been for a feafon,
during the preceding conteft. Let us examine
the following proofs :

Years.	Ships cleared outwards.			Value of cargoes.
1700	Tons Englifh.	D° foreign.	Total.	£.
1 }	273,693 -	43,635 -	317,328 -	6,045,432
2				
1705	——	——	——	5,308,966
1709	243,693 -	45,625 -	289,318 -	5,913,357
1711	266,047 -	57,890 -	323,937 -	5,962,988
1712	326,620 -	29,115 -	355,735 -	6,868,840

The revenue of the poft-office *, on an
average of the four laft years of
William, yielded nett — — £. 82,319
Ditto of the four firft years of the war - 61,568

* Mr. Aftle's Tranfcript.

Thus,

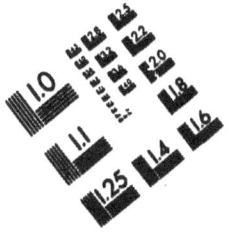

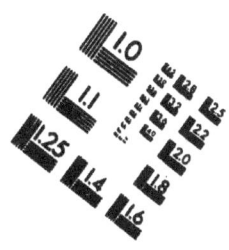

**IMAGE EVALUATION
TEST TARGET (MT-3)**

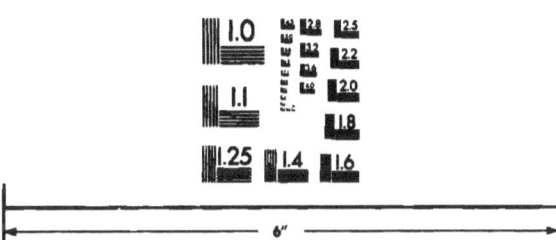

6"

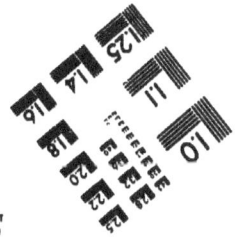

Photographic
Sciences
Corporation

23 WEST MAIN STREET
WEBSTER, N.Y. 14580
(716) 872-4503

Thus, the year 1705 marked the lowest stage of the depression of *commerce*, during Queen Anne's wars; whence it gradually rose till 1712, the last year of hostilities: when our navigation and traffic had gained a manifest superiority over those of any former period of peace.

Let us behold the rebound of this mighty spring, when the return of tranquillity had removed every pressure, by contrasting the average of the ships cleared outwards, and of the value of their cargoes, during the three peaceful years preceding the war, with both, during the three years immediately following the treaty of Utrecht.

Years.	Ships cleared outwards.			Value of cargoes.
	Tons, English.	D° foreign.	Total.	£.
1699 1700 1 }	393,703 -	43,625 -	347,328 -	6,709,881
1712 14 13 }	421,431 -	26,573 -	448,004 -	7,696,573

The nett annual revenue * of the post-
office, according to an average of the
years 1707—8—9—10 — £. 58,052

Ditto on an average † of the years
1711—12—13—14 — — 90,223

* Mr. Astle's Transcript.

† And. Chron. Com. vol. ii. p. 266: But, the office had been now extended to every dominion of the crown, and the rates of postage augmented one-third from 1710. The post-office revenue, says Anderson, is a kind of *politico-commercial pulse* of a nation's prosperity or decline.

At

Anglia in stead of that marvellous influence in manufactures, traffic, and industry, the people who ought to thrive... excited among them. Of these ... ... William Wood ... King George's ... expiring; our foreign commerce ... ... in general suspended; what little was left us ... precarious ... called ... ... in the ... by ... his dedication, he attributes our regeneration from "the lost condition which trade was then in, to His Majesty's timely accession." The ministers of this monarch did little ... to terminate ... by inciting all the clamour, or by propagating so much factious falshood. It was not the power of Ireland, which promoted the ... prosperity of our commercial affairs; but, it was peace.

The public revenue had now been divided into the ... ..., as the inland duties, the excise, and the customs; and into ... grants, as the malt and the land tax. The inland duties, confisting at the demise of the Queen, of fifteen distinct heads, were all managed by distinct commissioners, and may be estimated at the yearly amount of £.453,002, from an average of the years 1707—8—9—10. The ... property so

*. Wood's Dedication of The Survey of Trade. For this, Wood, was rewarded with the patent for coining Irish half-pence, which procured him so much ... of by Swift, and with what was of more ... value, the office of Secretary to the Commissioners of the Customs.

G   called,

called, and collected under the peculiar management of the commissioners of excise, consisted of twenty-seven different articles, and may be calculated, from the same average, at £ 1,462,945, including the duty on malt. And we may thence determine how much it may have obstructed labour, and checked the progress of population. The new customs, arising from our imports and exports, consisted then of forty-one different branches, and may be calculated from a fifteen years average, from 1700 to 1714 inclusive, to have amounted to £ 1,352,764 [*]. "

Having enumerated " that sad detail of taxes," the historian of our debts exclaims: " Can we wonder at the decay of our commerce, under such circumstances? Should not we rather wonder that we have any left?" But, what regard is there due to a general inference, in opposition to authentic facts? It has been already demonstrated, that in no former effluxion of time, did the manufactures and trade of England flourish so much, or amount to so large an extent, as at the demise of Queen Anne, notwithstanding the greatness of our imposts, and the immensity of our debts. And, when we consider too, that the taxes had produced abundantly, we may from these decisive circumstances certainly conclude, that the war had little incommoded the industrious classes; and that the principle of procreation exerted its powers, while an attentive diligence preserved a numerous pro-

* Philips's State of the Nation, p. 26.

geny,

geny, by furnishing the constant means of subsistence.

Whoever examines the laws of Queen Anne, with a view to this subject, must be of opinion, that they all tended to promote the commercial interests of the nation, as such interests were then understood.

But, the union of the two kingdoms is the glory, and ought to be the boast of her reign. The incorporation of two independent legislatures has proved equally advantageous to both countries, whether we regard the interest of the state, or the happiness of the governed. When we consider the weakness, which resulted from the ancient inroads of the Scotch, and the danger of future separation, we must allow, that this conjunction was worth to England almost any price. And the compression of the hearts and hands of two divided nations, gave an elasticity and vigour to the united kingdoms, which separately neither had ever attained. If as communities so much strength and felicity were derived from the Union, the Scotch, as individuals at least, were still greater gainers from this association of interests and affections. Freed from the tyranny of the nobles, by being admitted into a political system more liberal than their own, the people of Scotland thenceforth enjoyed the same privileges, as similar ranks in England had long derived from fortunate events, or wise institutions. And, invested with the same benefits of commerce, the Scotch melio-

rated

rated their agriculture, improved their manufactures, extended their trade, and acquired an opulence, which, as a people, feparate and overfha-
dowed, they had not for ages accomplifhed. The
acquifitions of both happily proved advantageous
to each. And while the Englifh bufily cultivated
the peculiar arts of peace, the Scotch were
brought, by a wife policy, from mountains, the
natural nurfery of warriors, to fight the national
battles of both.

From the epoch of the Union, the fame falutary regulations promoted equally the profperity
and populoufnefs of Great-Britain. Among thefe
Anderfon * has recorded the ufeful revifal, in
1710, of the ancient affize of bread and ale
[1266]; becaufe "it was fo neceffary for our
labourers and artificers, as well as for all other
people." Whatever number of lives were loft
during the wars of William and Anne, it feems
certain, fays that induftrious compiler, "that the
artificers of England did irreparable damage in
the mean time to the French, by robbing them
of many of their beft manufactures, wherewith
they had before fupplied almoft all Europe."

The foregoing details caft a juft cenfure on the
furious party-contefts, during the laft years of
Queen Anne, in refpect to the condition of our
commerce; as if the profperity, or the ruin of
manufactories and trade, were influenced by the

* Chron. Com. vol. ii. p. 251.

continuance

continuance of ftatefmen in the poffeffion, or in the
expectation, of emolument and power. The hufbandman and the failor only look for employment,
the mechanic and the merchant only inquire for
cuftomers, without caring who are the rulers, from
whom they enjoy protection, fince they feldom
gain from the contefts of the great.

WHILE George I. was in fecret little anxious
about the ftability of his throne, amid the clafh
of domeftic parties, he engaged fucceffively in
contefts with almoft every European power, becaufe each in its turn had given protection to the
Pretender to his crown.

But, the foreign difputes of this reign were fhort,
as well as unexpenfive. And they did not, therefore, call forth the whole force of the kingdom;
which may be deduced in the following manner.

If the current of population continued its progrefs, as we have feen it did to the commencement of the prefent reign, the fighting men muft
have amounted, during the time of George I. to
two millions and fifty thoufand. And the effective
wealth of the country, there is reafon to think,
had accumulated mean while in a ftill greater proportion.

Owing to the encreafe of circulation, which
enables the opulent to convert fo eafily land into
coin, or coin into land, and to the accumulation
too of moveable property, the intereft of money

began

began to fall towards the end of King William's
reign, when no great balance of trade flowed into
the kingdom. And the natural interest continuing low, even amid the preſſures of the ſubſequent
war, the Parliament enacted, in 1713, that the
legal intereſt ſhould not riſe higher than five per
cent. after September 1714. Thus England,
while ſhe was yet embarraſſed with the never-failing conſequences of war, gained " that abate-
ment of intereſt by law," which Sir Joſiah Child
rather too fondly inſiſted, during the preceding
age, would produce ſo many benefits to his country : The *advance of the price of lands in the purchaſe* ; the *improvement of the rent of farms* ; the
employment of the poor ; the *multiplication of artificers* ; the *increaſe of foreign trade* ; and the *augmentation of the ſtocks of people*. The natural intereſt of money fell to three per cent. in the reign
of George I. while the government ſeldom borrowed at more than four.

The practice of borrowing on behalf of the
ſtate had commenced with the preſſures of King
William's reign. This policy was continued, and
extended, during the wars of Anne. But, in the
time of her ſucceſſor, the contract between the
government and the lenders was not ſo much
made, as in preceding times, for the re-payment
of the principal, as for an annuity inſtead of intereſt.

The

The nation had thus contracted a debt, before
the 31st of December 1714, of - £. 50,644,307 ;
to pay the interest of which re-
quired, from the land and labour
of this kingdom - - - £. 2,811,904.

It ought to be remembered, however, that this
debt was due by the nation in its collective capacity ; but, that individual creditors had acquired
a vast capital in it, of the more importance to
them and the public ; as, besides yielding an annual profit, it was equally commodious as coin,
for all the uses of life ; since it could be easily
pledged, or transferred. And landowners were
thereby enabled to improve their estates, manufacturers to carry on their business, traders to extend our commerce, and every one to pay their
taxes. If by this debt, and by this annuity, the
state was somewhat embarrassed, the industrious
classes derived, probably, some advantage, from
the active motion, which was thereby given to the
circulating value of all things. Yet, if the people received no positive benefit, they were at least
enabled, by this facility, to sustain actual burdens
with greater ease.

While taxes were, without rigour, collected
from annual income, and not from productive capital, a financial operation was performed, in 1716,
which gradually relieved the embarrassments of

the

the ſtate, and gave freſh vigour to *circulation*, that
energetic principle of commercial times. All thoſe
taxes, which had from time to time been granted
for the payment of various annuities, were at once
made perpetual, and directed to be paid into three
great funds. The intereſt of the public debts was
reduced from ſix per cent. to five. And whatever
ſurpluſes might remain, after paying this liquidated intereſt, were ordered to be thrown into a
fourth fund, which was thenceforth called *the
ſinking fund*, becauſe it was deſigned to pay off
the principal and intereſt of ſuch debts, as had
been contracted before Chriſtmas 1716.

So productive were the taxes, owing to the
proſperity of the people, that theſe ſurpluſes
amounted, before the end of the reign of George I.
to £. 1,083,190 *. And theſe ſurpluſes would
have made the country ſtill more proſperous, had
the ſinking fund been conſtantly applied, as it was
thus originally deſigned; by keeping circulation
full and overflowing, and thereby preventing what
is commonly deplored as *a ſcarcity of money*.

Notwithſtanding that ſalutary operation, and
our manufactures and trade were at the ſame time
greatly encouraged, the capital of the public debts
amounted to nearly as much as in 1714 at the demiſe of George I. though the annuity, payable on
them, was by thoſe means reduced £. 1,133,807,

* Exchequer account, in the Hiſtory of Debts.

We

We shall however gain a more adequate idea, not only of the public revenue and burdens, but of the resources of the nation, from the following detail:

The nett excise, according to a medium of four years, ending at Michaelmas 1726 (exclusive of the malt-tax) - -	£.1,927,354	
The nett annual customs	1,530,361	
Various and promiscuous internal taxes -	666,459	
Total appropriated		£.4,124,175
The land-tax at 2 s. in the pound is given for	£.1,000,000	
Malt - duty brings in £.680,000, but is given for - -	750,000	
Raised by lottery - -	750,000	
Total annual grants for current services		2,500,000
Nett annual revenue - -		£.6,624,175
Charges of collection -		600,000
The gross sum raised yearly on the people - -		£.7,224,175

The

The public expenditure was as follows :

Interest of a debt of £. 50,793,555, including the surplus of the civil lift, which is 3,678 per annum,

	£. 2,240,985
The civil lift	800,000
	3,040,985
Surplus of the finking fund -	1,083,190
The current fervices of the army, navy, &c.	2,500,000
The annual charges with current fervices	6,624,175
Salaries and other charges, at leaft	600,000

Grofs fum annually applied - £. 7,224,175

The value of the furplus products of the land and labour of England, after domeftic confumption was fully fupplied, amounted yearly, at the acceffion of George I. to £. 8,008,068; which formed a much larger cargo than had ever been exported before. And from this circumftance we might infer, that there was now employed a greater capital in trade than, by means of its productive employment, had, in any prior age, promoted the wealth and greatnefs of Britain.

The English shipping, which exported that vast cargo, at the accession of George I. had then increased to - - - - 444,843 tons; which must have been navigated, if we allow twelve mariners to every two hundred tons, by - 26,691 men.

The royal navy, which had been principally left by Queen Anne, carried, in 1715 - - - 167,596 tons. Wood stated * the amount of the navy, in 1721, at - - - 158,233 tons; which, said he, is more than in 1688, by 57,201 tons; and more than in 1660, by 95,639.

Notwithstanding the boasts of Wood, and the glory acquired by defeating the Spanish fleet in 1718, it is apparent, that the navy had lately sustained a diminution of - - - 9,363 tons.

Having said thus much with regard to the strength of Britain, let us now examine the losses of our trade, from the petty wars of the present reign; which seem not indeed to have much interrupted the foreign commerce of the kingdom,

* Survey of Trade, p. 55.

while

while salutary regulations incited the domestic industry of the people.

Owing probably to a complication of causes,
the traffic and navigation of England appear to
have struggled with their oppressions; but never
to have risen much superior to the amount of both,
during the year of the accession of George I. The
following details offer sufficient proofs of this:

		Ships cleared outwards.		Value of cargoes.
Years.	Tons English.	Do foreign.	Total.	£.
1714	444,843 -	33,950 -	478,793 -	8,008,068
15	406,392 -	19,508 -	425,900 -	6,922,263
16	438,816 -	17,493 -	456,309 -	7,049,992
1718	427,962 -	16,809 -	444,771 -	6,361,390
23	392,643 -	27,040 -	419,683 -	7,395,908

We shall see however a progress, if we contrast
the averages of our navigation and trade, at the
beginning and at the end of George I's reign;
and if we also recollect, that the business of 1716
and 1727 was somewhat intercepted by war, or
by preparations for war.

		Ships cleared outwards.		Value of cargoes.
Years.	Tons English.	Do foreign.	Total.	£.
1713 14 15 }	421,431 -	26,573 -	448,004 -	7,696,573
1726 27 28 }	432,832 -	23,651 -	456,483 -	7,891,739

During

During this progress there were, however, "a general complaint and concern of the nation, on the subject of a decline of trade*." Joshua Gee published, about the same time, his treatise, in order "to shew the wounds our commerce and manufactories had received;" which "he put into the hands of the ministers, of the King, the Queen, and the Prince†." When Erasmus Philips wrote his State of the Nation, in 1725‡, he found "some men so gloomy, that they thought us in a worse condition than we really are, and that it would be impossible to pay off the public debts; since all this pomp is nothing but false lustre; as we owe more than we are worth; as our money is diminished; and, as we have little left but paper-credit." Against this contemporaneous declamation, which shews that man, in every age, utters his lamentations in a similar tone, Philips stated, what experience has shewn to have been undoubtedly true, the certain proofs of the prosperity and opulence of a country; great numbers of industrious people; a rich commonalty; money at low interest; and land at a great value.

Nevertheless, there were assuredly events, during the reign of George I, which cast a gloom over the nation, and obstructed general prosperity.

---

* Wood's Survey.   † Gee's Dedication.

‡ Preface to The State of the Nation; which, as well as Wood's Survey, was dedicated to the King, according to the practice of the times.

The

The persecutions of the great, on the accession of a new family, which were followed by the tumults of the mean, ought to give a lesson of moderation; since they were attended with no good consequences to the state. The subsequent rebellion of 1715 brought with it a twelvemonth of distraction, without leaving the terrors of example. And the war with Spain, in 1718, obstructed our Mediterranean commerce, as every war with that kingdom must continue to do, while the great cause of hostilities remains, and bids the Spaniards defiance. But, it was the infamous year 1720, which diverted all classes to projects and bubbles, that ought to be blotted from our annals, if they did not form remarkable beacons to direct our future course.

Of this reign it is the characteristic, that though in no period were there so many laws enacted, for promoting domestic and foreign trade, yet, at no time did both prosper less, during those days of captious peace, rather than avowed hostilities. The treaty of commerce with Spain, in 1715, must have inspired our traders with fresh vigour. The law which, in 1718, prohibited any British subject from carrying on traffic to the East under foreign commissions, turned their ardour upon more invigorating objects, by preventing productive capital from being sent abroad. The measure of allowing the exportation of *British-made linen, duty-free*, in 1717, gave us a manufacture, which

which is said, even then, to have employed many
thousands of the poor. And the fisheries were
encouraged by bounties, which must have multiplied the important race of our mariners.

The salutary laws, which were made for inciting domestic industry, were doubtless more efficacious in the subsequent reign, than they were felt
in any great degree, during the present. The manufactories of iron, of brass, and of copper, being
considered as the third in extent, since they employed, *as it is said*, in 1719, two hundred and
thirty thousand persons, were promoted with the
attention, which was due to their importance.
The continued encouragement, that had been given to the fabrics of silk, and the erection of the
vast machine of Lomb, in 1719, had raised the
annual value of this manufacture to £.700,000,
in 1722, more, as it is stated, than it had yielded at the Revolution.

But, the year 1722 must always form an epoch,
as memorable for a great operation in commercial
policy, as the establishment of the sinking fund
had been in finance, a few years before. The Parliament had indeed, in 1672, withdrawn the duties,
which were then payable by *aliens*, on the exportation of *our own* manufactures. This salutary
principle was still more extended, in 1700, by
removing the imposts on every kind of woollen
goods, that should be thereafter sent abroad. It
was however by the law *for the further encourage-*

ment

ment of manufactures, that every one was allowed
to export duty-free all merchandizes, the produce
of Great Britain, except only such articles as
should be deemed materials of manufacture; while
drugs, and other goods used for dying, were equally permitted to be imported duty-free. And other
facilities were at the same time given to trade,
whilst the fisheries were incited by bounties.

After enumerating all preceding measures of encouragement, Anderson * remarks, in 1727, that
nothing can more obviously demonstrate the ama-
zing increase of England's commerce, in less than
two centuries past, than the great growth of its
manufacturing towns, such as Liverpool, Manchester, Birmingham, and others; which are still
increasing in wealth, people, business, and buildings. Yet, Lord Molesworth † complained, in
1721, " that we are not one-third peopled, and
our stock of men daily decreases through our
wars, plantations, and sea-voyages." His lord-
ship was arguing, when he made this observation, for a general naturalization, a policy of very
doubtful merit, because in all sudden change there
is considerable inconvenience; and he may have
therefore been biassed by his principle. If this
nobleman intended to add his testimony to an apparent fact, that he saw no labourers to hire, his

* Chron. Com. vol. ii. p. 514.
† Pref. to his translation of Hottoman's Franco-Gallia,
2d edit. p. 23—4.

evidence

evidence would only prove, *that the induftrious claffes were fully employed*; and employment never fails to promote population. If his lordſhip only meant to give vent to his laudable anxieties for his country, this circumſtance would lead us to infer, that great as well as little minds are too apt to complain of the miferies of the prefent.

───────

THE reign of George II. with whatever finiſter events it opened, will be found to have promoted greatly, before its fuccefsful end, the induſtry and productive capital of the nation; and confequently, the efficient numbers of the people.

He found his kingdom burdened with a funded debt of rather more than fifty millions; which required, from the land and labour of the nation, taxes to the amount of two millions and upwards, to pay the creditors' annuity.

But, as his predeceffor reduced, ten years before, the intereft payable on the public debts, from fix *per cent.* to five, the adminiſtration of the prefent King made a further reduction, with the confent of all parties, from five *per cent.* to four, in 1727. Thefe meafures, which the fortunate circumſtances of the times rendered eafy and fafe, not only ſtrengthened public and private credit, but, by reducing the natural intereft of money ſtill more, muſt have thereby facilitated every operation

H   ration

ration of domeſtic manufactures, as well as every
effort of foreign traffic. The fabrics of wool
were at the ſame time freed from fraud. And
the peace with Spain, in 1728, muſt have invigorated our exportations to the Mediterranean ; the
more, as a truce was then alſo made with Morocco.

Yet, party-rage ran ſo high, in 1729, ſays An-
derſon *, that the friends of the miniſter found
themſelves obliged to prove by *facts*, what was
before generally known to be true, that *Britain
was then in a thriving condition*: the low intereſt
of money, ſaid they, demonſtrates a greater plenty of caſh than formerly ; this abundance of money has raiſed the price of lands from twenty and
twenty-one years purchaſe to twenty and twenty-
five ; which proves, that there were more perſons
able and ready to buy than formerly :—And the
great ſums of late expended in the incloſing and
improving of lands, and in opening mines, are
proofs of an augmentation of opulence and people ; while the increaſed value of our exports
ſhews an increaſe of manufactures, and the greater

* Chron. Com. vol. ii. p. 322.—The cauſe of the above-
mentioned *party-rage* is now ſufficiently known. Sir Spencer
Compton outwitted himſelf in the bargain for *place*, about
Queen Caroline's jointure. Sir R. Walpole did not higgle
with her Majeſty about a hundred thouſand pounds : and he
was, in return, continued *the miniſter*. But, the proſperity
of the people is no wiſe connected with the intereſted conteſts
among *the great*.

number

number of shipping cleared outwards marks the greater extent of our navigation.

If we compare the averages of our veffels and cargoes, in the firft years of the prefent reign, with thofe of the three years of peace, which preceded the war of 1739, we shall fee all thefe truths in a still more pleafing light.

Years.	Ships cleared outwards.			Value of cargoes.
	Tons Eng.	D° foreign.	Total.	£.
1726 27 28	432,832 -	23,651 -	456,483 -	7,918,406
1736 37 38	476,941 -	26,627 -	503,568 -	9,993,232

It was at this moment of unexampled profperity, that the elder Lord Lyttelton wrote *Confiderations on the prefent State of Affairs*, (1738). " In moft parts of England," fays he, " gentlemen's rents are fo ill paid, and the weight of taxes lies fo heavy upon them, that thofe who have nothing from the Court can fcarce fupport their families.—Such is the ftate of our manufactures, fuch is that of our colonies; both fhould be enquired into, that the nation may know, whether the former can fupport themfelves much longer under their various preffures." The editor of his lordfhip's works would have done no differvice to the memory of a worthy man, had he configned this factious effufion to anonymous obfcurity. Animated by a congenial fpirit, Pope too wrote *Confiderations on the State of Affairs;* in his two dialogues, entitled THIRTY-EIGHT, he reprefents, in moft energetic language, and exquifite numbers, the nation *as totally ruined ;* as *overwhelmed with corruption.* It was about the fame time alfo, that Sir Mathew Decker compofed his effay " *On the Caufes of the Decline of Foreign Trade."* But, it is not eafy to conceive any difquifition more depraved, than a treatife to explain *the caufes of an effect* which did *not exift.*

It was the evident purpofe of fome of thefe writers to drive the nation headlong into war, without thinking of any other confequences, than acquiring power, or gratifying fpleen ; and without caring how much a people, reprefented as unable to pay their rents, might be burthened with taxes ; or a country, painted as feeble from diffipation, might be difgraced, or conquered.

If the nation had thus profpered in her affairs, and the people thus increafed in their numbers, Great Britain muft have contained, when fhe was factioufly forced, into war with Spain, a greater number of fighting men, than had ever fought her battles before. And fhe, muft have poffeffed a mafs of productive capital, and a greatnefs of annual income, far fuperior to thofe of former years.

The courfe of circulation had filled, and even overflowed. The natural intereft of money ran fteadily at three per cent. The price of all the public fic securities had risen so much higher than they had been in any other period, that the three *per cent.* stocks sold at a premium on 'Change *. And the annual surpluses of the standing taxes, as they were paid into the finking-fund, amounted, in 1738, to no less a sum than £. 1,231,127.

Of this fund it has been very properly observed, that while it contributes to the liquidation of former debts, it still more facilitates the contracting of new ones. But, the great contest among the public creditors at that fortunate epoch, was not so much who should be paid his capital, but who should be suffered to remain creditors of the state †.

The value of the surplus produce of our land and labour, which were then exported, amounted yearly to £. 9,993,232; and which might have been applied, when sent to foreign countries, as remittances for carrying on the war at the greatest distance. It is indeed an acknowledged fact, that during no effluxion of time was there ever such considerable balances paid to England, as there were transmitted in the course of the war of 1739, on the general state of her payments.

The English shipping, which actually transported that vast cargo, amounted annually to 476,941 tons; which were navigated probably by 26,616 men, who might have been all engaged in the public service, either by influence, or force.

_____

* Sir J. Barnard's speech for the reduction of interest.   † Id.

H 3   There

There had mean while been an equal progrefs in the royal navy; which carried

	Tons.
in 1727 — —	170,862
in 1741 — —	198,387
in 1749 — —	208,215 *

Thus much being premifed, as to the ftate of our ftrength, we fhall gain a fufficient knowledge of the condition of our navigation and commerce, during the war of 1739, by attending to the fub-joined detail:

* An admiralty-lift, in the Paper-office, gives us the following detail of the King's fhips in fea-pay, on the 19th July 1738.

	Ships.		
Stationed in the Plantations -	24	carrying	5,045 men,
in the Mediterranean,	17	- -	5,011
at Newfoundland,	3	- -	690
Ordered home, -	4	- -	720
On the Irifh coaft, - -	6	- -	350
At home, - - - -	41	- -	9,602
	95	-	23,418 mariners.

By preparations for a naval war, the foregoing lift had been fwelled, before March 1739, to 147 fhips, carrying 38,849 men. But their numbers were defective, in 4,758 borne, and in 8,618 muftered.—From the fame authority, we have the following abftract of the royal navy in June 1748; which, when compared with the lift of 1738, gives us an idea fufficiently precife of *the fleet* of England, during the war of 1739.

It confifted of - - - 89 fhips of the line.
of - - - - 153 frigates.

242; whofe complement of men was 60,654.

Years.	Ships cleared outwards.			Value of cargoes.
	Tons Englifh.	D° foreign.	Total.	£.
1736 37 38	476,941 -	26,627 -	503,568 -	9,993,232
1739 40 41	384,191 -	87,260 -	471,451 -	8,870,499
1744	373,817 -	72,849 -	446,666 -	9,190,621
1747	394,571 -	101,671 -	496,242 -	9,775,340
1748	479,236 -	75,477 -	554,713 -	11,141,202

Thus the year 1744 marked the ultimate point of commercial depreffion, if we judge from the tonnage; and 1740, if we draw our inference from the value of exports: Yet, whether we argue from the one or the other, we muft conclude, that the intereft of merchants was little affected by this naval war.

But, we fhall at once fee how little our induftrious claffes were affected, by the war, at home, and with what elafticity the fpring of foreign trade rebounded on the removal of warfare, by comparing the averages of our navigation and commerce, during the peaceful years before hoftilities began, and after they ended:

Years.	Ships cleared outwards.			Value of cargoes.
	Tons Englifh.	D° foreign.	Total.	£.
1736 37 38	476,941 -	26,627 -	503,568 -	9,993,232
1749 50 51	609,798 -	51,386 -	661,184 -	12,599,112

During

During the foregoing fifty years of uncommon profperity, as to our agriculture * and manufacture, our navigation, and traffic, and credit, the incumbrances of the public, and the burdens of the people, equally continued to increafe. The debt, which was left at the demife of Queen Anne, remained undiminifhed in its capital at the demife of George I. though the annuity payable on it had been leffened almoft a million. The ten years of fubfequent peace having made little alteration, the public debt amounted, on the 31ft of December 1738, to - £. 46,314,829. 10s. 0½d. on the 31ft of December 1749 to - - † 74,221,686. 10s. 11½d. :

—whence we perceive, by an eafy calculation, that an additional debt had been mean while incurred, of £. 27,906,857. 0s. 11 d. befides un-

* It appears, by an account laid before the Parliament, that there had been exported in *five* years, from 1744 to 1748, *corn* from England to the amount of 3,768,444 quarters; which, at a medium of prices, was worth to this nation, £. 8,007,948. Now, the average of the five years is 753,689 quarters yearly, of the value of £.1,601,589. The exportation of 1749 and 1750 rose ftill higher. "This is an immenfe fum," fays the compiler of the Annual Regifter, [1772, p. 197] "to flow immediately from the produce of the earth, and the labour of the people; enriching our merchants, and increafing an invaluable breed of feamen." He might have added, with equal propriety, *enriching our yeomanry, and increafing the ufeful breed of labourers dependant on them.*

† Hiftory of Debts.

funded

funded debts to a confiderable amount, But, the nine years war of 1739 coft this nation upwards of fixty-four millions, without gaining an object; becaufe no valuable object can be gained by any war. It is to be lamented, when hoftilities ceafe, that the party, which forces the nation to begin them, without adequate caufe, is not compelled to pay the expence.

The current of wealth, which had flowed into the nation, during the obftructions of war, continued a ftill more rapid courfe, on the return of peace. The taxes produced abundantly, becaufe an induftrious people confumed liberally. And the furplufes of all the impofts, after paying the intereft of debts, amounted to £. 1,274,172 [*]. The coffers of the rich began to overflow. Circulation became ftill more rapid. The intereft of money, which had rifen during the preffures of war to four *per cent.* fell to three, when the ceffation of hoftilies terminated the loans to government. The adminiftration feized this profperous moment to reduce, with the confent of the proprietors, the intereft of almoft fifty-eight million of debts from four *per cent.* to three and a half, for feven years, from 1750, and afterwards to three *per cent.* for ever. And by thefe prudent meafures, the annuity payable to the creditors of the ftate was leffened, in the years 1750 and 1751, from £. 2,966,000 to £. 2,663,000 [†].

[*] Hiftory of Debts from an Exchequer account.
[†] J. Poftlethwayt's Hiftory of the Revenue, p. 238.

It

It was at this fortunate epoch, that Lord Bolingbroke wrote *Some Considerations on the State of the Nation*; in which he represents *the public as on the verge of bankruptcy*, and *the people as ready to fall into confusion*, from their *distress* and *danger*. Little did that illustrious party-man know, at least little was he willing to own, how much both the public and the people had advanced, from the time when he had been driven from power, in all that can make a nation prosperous and great. Doddington at the same time—" faw the country in so dangerous a condition, and found himself so incapable to give it relief *,"—that he resigned a lucrative office from pure disinterestedness. And the second edition of Decker's *Essay on the Causes of the Decline of Foreign Trade*, was opportunely published, with additional arguments, in 1750, to evince to the world the *causes* of an *effect*, that did *not exist*.

Notwithstanding all that apparent prosperity and augmentation of numbers, we ought to mention, as circumstances, which probably may have retarded the progress of population, the Spanish war of 1727, that was not, however, of long continuance. The settlement of Georgia, in 1733, carried off a few of the lowest orders, the idle and the needy. The real hostilities that began in 1739, were probably attended with much more baneful consequences. The rebellion of 1745, introduced a temporary disorder, though

* Diary, March 1749—50, &c.

there

there were drawn from its confusions, measures
the most salutary, in respect to industry and population. " Let the country gentlemen," says Cor-
byn Morris, when speaking on the then mortality
of London [March 1750-1] " be called forth
and declare—Have they not continually felt, for
many years past, an increasing want of husband-
men and day-labourers ? Have the farmers
throughout the kingdom no just complaints of the
excessive increasing prices of workmen, and of the im-
possibility of procuring a sufficient number at any
price ?"

Now, admitting the truth of these pregnant af-
firmations, they may be shewn to have been altogether consistent with facts and with principles.
Allowing his *many years* to reach to the demise of
George I. it may be asserted, because it has been
proved, that our agriculture had been so much
improved, as not only to supply domestic wants,
but even to furnish other nations with the means
of subsistence ; and every branch of our manufactures kept pace with the flourishing state of our
husbandry. It is surely demonstrable, that it required a greater number of artificers to manufacture commodities of the value of £. 11,141,202,
and to navigate 554,713 tons of shipping, in
1748, than to fabricate goods of the value of
£. 7,951,772, and to navigate 456,483 tons of
shipping, in 1728. But, great demand creates a
scarcity of all things ; which in the end procures
an abundant supply. And, that *the excessive prices*

of

of workmen did in fact produce a reinforcement of *workmen,* may be inferred from the numbers which, in no long period, were brought into action, by public and private encouragement.

We fee in familiar life, that when money is expended upon works of uncommon magnitude; in any village, or parish, labourers are always collected, in proportion to the augmentation of employments. Experience shews, that the fame increase of the induſtrious claſſes never fails to enſue in larger diſtricts ; in a town, a county, or a kingdom, when proportional fums are expended for labour. And it is in this manner, that manufactures and trade every where augment the numbers of mankind, by the active expenditure of productive capitals. He, then, who labours to evince, that the lower orders of men decreaſe in numbers, while agriculture, the arts (both uſeful and ornamental) with commerce, are advancing from inconſiderable beginnings, to unexampled greatneſs, is only diligent to prove, That *cauſes do* NOT *produce their effects.*

To thoſe reaſons of proſperity, that, having for years exiſted, had thus produced the moſt beneficial effects, prior to the peace of Aix-la-Chapelle, new encouragements were immediately added. The reduction of the intereſt of the national debts, by meaſures altogether conſiſtent with juſtice and public faith, ſhewed not only the flouriſhing condition of the kingdom, but alſo tended to make it flouriſh ſtill more. And there neceſſarily followed

all

all thofe falutary confequences, in refpeet to domeftic diligence and foreign commerce, which, Sir
Jofiah Child infifted a century before, would refult from *the lownefs of intereft*.

An additional incitement was at the fame time
given to the whale-fifhery, partly by the naturalization of fkilful foreigners, but more by pecuniary
bounties. The eftablifhment of the corporation of
The Free Britifh Fifhery, in 1750, muft have promoted population, by giving employment to the
induftrious claffes, however unprofitable the projeet
may have been to the undertakers, whofe fuccefs was
unhappily fo unequal to their good intentions and
unrecompenfed expences. The voluntary fociety,
which was entered into in 1754, *for the Encouragement of Arts, Manufaetures, and Commerce*, muft have
been attended with ftill more beneficial effeets, by
animating the fpirit of experiment and perfeve-
rance. And the laws, which were fucceffively enaet-
ed, and meafures purfued, from 1732 to 1760, *for
preventing the exceffive ufe of fpirituous liquors*, muft
have promoted populoufnefs, by preferving the
health, and inciting the diligence of the lower orders of the people.

Yet, thefe ftatutes, falutary as they muft have
been, did promote the health and numbers of the
people, in a more eminent degree, than the laws
which were paffed, during the fame period, for
making more eafy communications by the improvement of roads. We may judge of the neceffity of thefe acts of legiflation from the penalties
annexed

annexed to them. Of the founderous condition of the roads of England, while they were amended by the compulsive labour of the poor, we may judge indeed from the wretched state of the ways, which, in the present times, are kept in repair by the ancient mode. Turnpikes, which we saw first introduced soon after the Restoration, were erected slowly, in opposition to the prejudices of the people. The act, which for a time made it felony, at the beginning of the reign of George II. to pull down a toll-gate, was continued as a perpetual law, before the conclusion of it. Yet, the great roads of England remained almost in their ancient condition, even as late as 1752 and 1754, when the traveller seldom saw a turnpike for two hundred miles, after leaving the vicinity of London *. And we now know from experience how much the making of highways and bridges advances the population of any country, by extending correspondence, by facilitating communications, and, consequently, by promoting internal traffic, which was thereby rendered greater than our foreign; since *the best customers of Britain are the people of Britain.*

AFTER a captious peace of very short duration, the flames of war, which for several years had burnt unseen among the American woods, broke out at length in 1755. Unfortunate as

* See the Gentleman's Magazine 1752—54.

these

(111)

thefe hoftilities were at the beginning, they yet proved fuccefsful in the end, owing to caufes, that it is the province of hiftory to explain.

However fafhionable it then was for difcontented ftatefmen to talk * of *the confuming condition of the country*, it might have been inferred beforehand, that we had prodigious refources, if the ruling powers had been animated by any genius. The defeats, which plainly followed from mifconduct, naturally brought talents of every kind into action. And the events of the war of 1755 convinced the world, notwithftanding every *eftimate* of the *manners* and *principles* of *the times*, that the ftrength of Great-Britain is irrefiftible, when it is conducted with fecrecy and difpatch, with wifdom and energy.

When Brackenridge was upbraided by Forfter, for making public degrading accounts of our population, at the commencement of the war of 1755, he afked, juftly enough, " *What encouragement can it give to the enemy to know, that we have two millions of fighting men in our Britifh iflands ?*" But we had affuredly in our Britifh iflands a million more than Brackenridge unwillingly allowed.

The *natural* intereft of money, which had been 3 *per cent.* at the beginning of this reign, never rofe higher than £.3. 13s. 6d. at the conclufion of it, after an expenfive courfe of eight years hoftilities. During the two firft years of the war, the minifters borrowed money at 3 *per cent.* But, five millions being lent to the adminiftration in 1757, the lenders required 4¼ *per cent.* And from the

* See Doddington's Diary, 1755—6—7.

former

former punctuality of government, and present ease with which taxes were found to pay the stipulated interest, Great Britain commanded the money of Europe, when the pressures of war obliged France to stop the payment of interest on some of her funded debts.

Mean time the surplufes of the standing taxes of Great Britain amounted, at the commencement of the war, to one million three hundred thousand pounds, which, after the reduction of the interest of debts in 1757, swelled to one million six hundred thousand pounds. And from this vast current of income, the more scanty streams, which slowly flowed from new imposts, were continually supplied.

It is the expences, more than the slaughter, of modern war, which debilitate every community. The whole supplies granted by Parliament, and raised upon the people, during the reign of George II. amounted * to £. 183,976,624.

The supplies granted, during the five years of the war, before the decease of that prince, amounted to   -   -   -   -   £. 54,319,325

The supplies voted, during the three first years of his successor, amounted † to -   -   . -   51,437,314

The principal expences of a war, which, having been undertaken to drive the French from North America, has proved unfortunate in the issue   -   -   £. 105,756,639

---

* Camp. Pol. Sur. vol. ii. p. 551.   † Id.

Yet,

Yet, none of the taxes that had been established, in order to raise those vast sums, bore heavy on the industrious classes, if we except the additional excise of three shillings a barrel on beer*. And, whatever burdens may have been imposed, internal industry pursued its occupations, and the enterprize of our traders sent to every quarter of the globe, merchandizes to an extent, beyond all example.

There were exported annually, during the first years of the war, surpluses of our land and labour,

* That the consumption of the great body of the people was not lessened in consequence of the war, we may certainly infer from the official details, in the Appendix to The Observations on the State of the Nation:

The average of eight years nett produce of the
duty on soap, &c. ending with 1754   -   £. 228,114
Ditto   -   -   ending with 1767   -   264,902

Ditto on candles, - ending with 1754   -   £. 136,073
Ditto on ditto, - ending with 1767 -   •   155,716

Ditto on hides, - ending with 1754 -   -   £. 188,400
Ditto on ditto, - ending with 1767 -   -   189,216

As no new duties had been laid on the before-mentioned necessaries of life, the augmentation of the revenue evinces an increase of consumption; consequently of comforts; and consequently of people. In confirmation, let it be considered too, that the *hereditary* and *temporary excise* produced, according to an eight years average, ending with 1754 - £.525,317.
Ditto ending with 1767   -   -   -   -   538,542.

I

to the amount of £. 11,708,515 *; which being sent abroad from time to time, to different markets, as demand required, might have been all applied, (as some of them undoubtedly were) in paying the fleets and armies, that spread terror over every hostile nation.

The English shipping, which after exporting that vast cargo might have been employed by government as transports, and certainly furnished the fleet with a hardy race, amounted to 609,798 tons; which must have been navigated, if

we allow twelve men to every 200
tons burden, by - - 36,588 men.

We may determine, with regard to the progress and magnitude of the royal navy, from the following statement:

	Tonnage.	Sailors voted by Parliament.	Their wages, &c.
In 1749 —	228,215 —	17,000 —	£. 839,800
1754 —	226,246 —	10,000 —	494,000
1760 —	300,416 —	70,000 —	3,458,000

It is the boast of Britain, "that while other countries suffered innumerable calamities, during that long period of hostilities, this happy island escaped them all; and cultivated, unmolested, her manufactures, her fisheries, and her commerce, to an amount, which has been the wonder and envy of the world." This flattering picture of Doctor Campbell will, however, appear to be ex-

* There were moreover exported from Scotland, according to an average of 1755—6—7, · - - - £. 663,401.

tremely

tremely like the original, from an examination of the fubfequent details; which are more accurate in their notices, and ftill more juft in their con- clufions. Compare, then, the following averages of our navigation and traffick, during the fubjoin- ed years, both of peace and war:

Years.	Tons Englifh.	Dº foreign.	Total.	Value of cargoes. £.
1749 50 51	609,798 -	51,386 -	661,184 -	12,599,112
1755 56 57	451,254 -	73,456 -	524,711 -	11,708,515
1760	471,241 -	112,737 -	573,978 -	14,693,270
61	508,220 -	117,835 -	626,055 -	14,873,194
62	480,444 -	120,126 -	600,570 -	13,546,171

Thus, the year 1756 marked the loweft point of the depreffion of commerce; whence it gra- dually rofe, till it had gained a fuperiority over the unexampled traffick of the tranquil years 1749-50- 51, if we may judge from the value of exports; and almoft to an equality, if we draw our infer- ences from the tonnage. The Spanifh war of 1762 impofed an additional weight, and we have feen the confequent decline.

When, by the treaty of Paris, entire freedom was again reftored to foreign commerce, the traders once more fent out adventures of a ftill greater amount to every quarter of the globe, though the nation was fuppofed to be ftrained by too great an exertion of its powers. The falutary effects of

I 2

more extenfive manufactures and a larger trade
were inftantly feen in the commercial fuperiority
of the three years following the pacification of
1763, over thofe enfuing the peace of 1748, tho'
thefe have been celebrated juftly as times of uncommon profperity. We fhall be fully convinced
of this fatisfactory truth, if we examine the following proofs :

Years.	Tons Englifh.	D° foreign.	Total.	Value of cargoes. £.
1749 50 51	609,798	51,386	661,184	12,599,112
1758	389,842	116,002	505,844	12,618,335
1759	406,335	121,016	527,351	13,947,788
1764 65 66	639,872	68,136	708,008	14,925,950

Ships cleared outwards.

The grofs income of the Poft-office, foreign and
domeftic, *which*, it is faid, *can alone demonftrate
the extent of our correfpondence*, amounted,

In 1754, to   -   -   £. 210,663
In 1764, to   -   :   281,535 *.

IT was at this fortunate epoch, that Great
Britain, having carried conqueft over the hoftile
powers of the earth, by her arms, faved Europe
from bankruptcy, by the fuperiority of her opulence, and by the difintereftednefs of her fpirit.

* The account of the Poft-office revenue is ftated, by the
Annual Regifter 1773, much higher, miftakingly.

The

The failures, which happened at Berlin, at Hamburgh, and in Holland, during July 1763, communicated difmay and diftruft to every commercial town, on the European continent *. Wealth, it is faid, no longer procured credit, or connection any more gained confidence: The merchants of Europe remained for fome time in confternation, becaufe every trader feared for himfelf, amidft the ruins of the greateft houfes. It was at this crifis, that the Britifh traders fhewed the greatnefs of their capitals, the extent of their credit, and how little they regarded either lofs or gain, while the mercantile world feemed to pafs away as a winter's cloud: They trufted correfpondents, whofe fituations were extremely unftable, to a greater amount than they had ever ventured to do, in the moft profperous times: And they made vaft remittances to thofe commercial cities, where the deepeft diftrefs was fuppofed to prevail, from the determination of the wealthieft bankers to fufpend the payment of their own acceptances. At this crifis the Bank of England difcounted bills of exchange to an incredible amount, while every bill was doubted. And the Britifh government, with a wife policy, actuated and fupported all †.

* See the defpondent letter from the bankers of Hamburgh to the bankers of Amfterdam, dated the 4th of Auguft 1763, In the Gentleman's Magazine of this year, p. 422.

† See Confiderations on the Trade and Finances of the Kingdom.

I 3 On

On this proud day was publifhed, however, "*An Alarm to the Stockholders*." By another writer the nation was remembered of " *the decreafe of the current coin, as a moft dangerous circumflance.*" And by an author, ftill more confiderable than either, we were inftructed—" How the abilities of the country were ftretched to their utmoft extent, and beyond their natural tone, whilft trade fuffered in proportion : For, the price both of labour and materials was enhanced by the number and weight of the new taxes, and by the extraordinary demand which the ruin of the French navigation brought on Great Britain ; whereby rival nations may be now enabled to under-fell us at foreign markets, and rival us in our own : That both public and private credit were at the fame time oppreffed by the rapid increafe of the national debt, by the fcarcity of money, and the high rate of intereft, which aggravated every evil, and affected every money tranfaction."—Such is the melancholic picture, which was exhibited of our fituation, foon after the peace of 1763, by the hand of a mafter *, who probably meant to fketch a caricature, rather than to draw a portrait.

If, however, the *refources* of Britain arife chiefly from the *labour* of Britain, it may be eafily fhewn, that there never exifted in this ifland fo many *induftrious people*, as at the return of peace in 1763. It is not eafy, indeed, to calculate the numbers, who

* Confiderations on the Trade and Finances of the Kingdom, p. 3.

die

die in the camp, or in battle, more than would
otherwise perish from want, or from vice, in the
city or hamlet. It is some confolation, that the
laborious claffes are too wealthy to covet the pit-
tance of the foldier, or too independent to court
the dangers of the failor. And though the for-
faken lover, or the reftlefs vagrant, may look for re-
fuge in the army or the fleet, it may admit of fome
doubt, how far the giving of proper employment to
both, may not have freed their parifhes from dif-
quietude and from crimes. There is, therefore,
no room, to fuppofe, that any one left the anvil,
or the loom, to follow *the idle trade of war*, during
the hoftilities of 1755, or that there were lefs private income and public circulation, after the re-
eftablifhment of peace, than at any prior epoch.
For, it muft undoubtedly have required a greater
number of artificers to produce merchandizes for
foreign exportation, after feeding and cloathing
the inhabitants, to the
value of   -   -   £.14,694,970 - in 1760,
than it did to fabricate
the value of   -   12,599,112 - in 1750.
It muft have demanded a
ftill greater number of
hands to work up goods
for exportation of the
value of   -   -   16,512,404 - in 1764,
than it did to manufacture
the value of   -   14,873,191 - in 1761.

I 4   A greater

A greater number of feamen muft furely have been employed to navigate and repair - - - 471,241 - in 1760, than - - - 451,254 - in 1756. And a ftill greater number to man and repair - 651,402 - in 1765, than - - - 609,798* - in 1750.

* It is acknowledged, that Scotland furnifhed a greater number of recruits for the fleets and armies of Britain, during the war of 1755, than England, confidering the fmaller number of her fighting men. Yet, by this drain, the induftrious claffes feem not to have been in the leaft diminifhed. For of linen there were made for fale,

  in 1758 - - 10,624,435 yards.
  in 1760 - - 11,747,728.

Of the augmentation of the whole products of Scotland during the war, we may judge from the following detail : The value of merchandizes exported from Scotland,

  in 1756 - - £. 663,401
    60 - - 1,086,205
    64 - - 1,243,927

There were exported yearly, of *British-manufactured* linens, according to an average of feven years of peace, from 1749 to 1755 - - - - 576,373 yards, Ditto, according to an average of feven years of fubfequent war, from 1756 to 1762 1,355,226.

Having thus difcovered that the fword had not been put into *ufeful* hands, let us take a view of the great woollen manufactories of England, with an afpect to the fame exhilarating fubject. The value of *woollen goods* exported,

  in 1755 - - £. 3,575,297
    57 - - 4,758,095
    58 - - 4,673,461
    59 - - 5,352,299
    60 - - 5,453,172

Yet,

Yet, it muſt be confeſſed, that however *the people* individually may have been employed, *the ſtate* corporately was embarraſſed in no ſmall degree, by the debts, which had been contracted by a war, glorious, but unprofitable. Upwards of fifty-eight millions had been added to our funded debts, before we began to negociate for peace in 1762. When the unfunded debts were afterwards brought to account, and aſſigned an annual intereſt, from a ſpecific fund, the whole debt, which was incurred, by the hoſtilities of 1755, ſwelled to £.72,111,000. And when every claim on the public, for the war's expences, was honeſtly ſatisfied, the national debt amounted to   ‑   ‑   £.146,682,844,

which yielded the creditors, to whom it was due, an annuity of   ‑   ‑   ‑   £.4,850,821.

Though it is the intereſt, and not the capital [*], that conſtitutes the real debt of *the ſtate*, yet this annuity

---

[*] Writers have been carried of late, by their zeal of patriotiſm, to demand the payment of the principal of the debt, though the intereſt be punctually paid; as if the nature of the contract between *the individual* and *the ſtate* had ſtipulated for the payment of both. The fact is, that few lenders, ſince King William's days, have expected repayment of *the capitals*, which they lent to the government. *The ſtocks*, as the public ſecurities of the Britiſh nation are called, may be compared to the money tranſactions of the Bank of Amſterdam, as they have been explained by Sir James Stewart. No man who lodges *treaſure* in this Bank, ever expects to ſee it again: But he may *tranſfer the Bank receipt* for it. The Directors of this

annuity was, doubtlefs, a heavy incumbrance on the land and labour of this ifland: And however burdenfome, it was not the only weight that obftructed, in whatever degree, the induftrious claffes, in adding accumulation to accumulation. The charge of the civil government was then calculated as an expence to the people of a million. And the peace eftablifhment, for the army, navy, and mifcellaneous fervices of lefs amount, though of as much ufe, may be ftated at three millions and a half, without entering into the controverfy of that changeful day, whether it was a few pounds more, or a few pounds lefs. If it aftonifhed Europe to fee Great Britain borrow, in *one* year, *twelve millions*, and to find taxes to pay the intereft of fuch a loan, amidft hoftilities of unbounded expence,

this Bank difcovered from experience, that if the number of *fellers* of thefe receipts fhould at any time be greater than the *buyers* of them, the value of *actual treafure fafely lodged* would depreciate. And it is fuppofed, that thefe prudent managers employ brokers to buy up the Bank receipts, when they begin to fall in their value, from the fuperabundance of them on 'Change. Apply this rational explanation to the Britifh funds. No creditor of a *funded debt* can afk payment of the principal at the Treafury; but, he may difpofe of his ftock in *the Alley*. The principles, which regulate demand and fupply, are equally applicable to the Britifh funds, as to *the treafure* in the Amfterdam Bank. If there are more fellers than buyers, the price of ftocks will fall: If there are more buyers than fellers, they will as naturally rife. And the time is now come, when the Britifh government ought to employ every pound, which can poffibly be faved, in buying up the *principal* of fuch public debts as prefs the moft.

it

it might have given the European world still higher ideas of the refources of Britain, to fee her fatisfy every claim, and re-eftablifh her financial affairs, in no long period after the conclufion of war.

But, the acquifitions of peace proved, unhappily, more embarraffing to the collective mafs of an induftrious nation, than the imports, which were conftantly collected, for paying the intereft of debts, and the charges of government. The treaty of 1763 retained Canada, Louifiana, and Florida, on the American continent; the Granades, Tobago, St. Vincent, and Dominica, in the Weft Indies; and Senegal in Africa. Without regarding other objects, here was a wide field opened for the attention of intereft, and for the operations of avarice. Every man, who had credit with the minifters at home, or influence over the governors in the colonies ran for the prize of American territory. And many land-owners in Great Britain, of no fmall importance, neglected the poffeffions of their fathers, for a portion of wildernefs, beyond the Atlantic. This was the fpirit, which formerly debilitated Spain, more than the Peruvian mines; becaufe the Spaniards turned their affections from their country to the Indies. With a fimilar fpirit, millions of productive capital were withdrawn from the agriculture, and manufactures, and trade of Great Britain, to cultivate the ceded iflands, in the other hemifphere. Domeftic occupations were obftructed confequently, and circulation was ftopped, in proportion to the

ftocks

ſtocks withdrawn, to the induſtry enfeebled, and to the ardour turned to leſs ſalutary objects.

While the collective maſs of the people were thus individually injured in their affairs, the ſtate ſuffered equally in its finances. The new acquiſitions required the charge of civil governments, which was provided for in the annual ſupplies, but from taxes on the land and labour of this iſland. To defend theſe acquiſitions, larger and more expenſive military eſtabliſhments became now neceſſary, though our conqueſts did not yield a penny in return *. And an additional drain being thus opened for the circulating money, the opulent men, who generally lend to government, enhanced the price of a commodity, which was thus rendered more valuable, by the inceſſant demands of adventurers, who offered the uſurious intereſt of the Indies †. The coins did not conſequently overflow the coffers of the rich; the price of the public funds did not riſe as at the former peace, when no ſuch drain exiſted; and the government was unable to make bargains for the public, in 1764, equally advantageous, as at the leſs ſplendid epoch of 1750.

In theſe views of an intereſting ſubject, the true objection to the peace of 1763 was not, that

---

* There were ſome ſmall ſums brought into the annual ſupplies from the ſale of lands in the ceded iſlands.

† It was a wiſe policy, therefore, to encourage foreigners to lend money on the ſecurity of Weſt India eſtates.

we

we had *retained too little*, but that we had *retained too much*. Had the French been altogether exclud-ed from the fisheries of Labrador and Newfound-land, and wholly reftored to every conqueft, the peace had been perhaps more complete. Whe-ther the minifters could have juftified fuch a trea-ty, within the walls of Parliament, or without, is a confideration perfonal to them, and is an ob-ject, quite diftinct in argument. Unhappy ! that a Britifh minifter, to defend himfelf from cla-mour, muft generally act againft the genuine inte-reft of his country.

Fortunate it is, however, for Britain, that there is a fpirit in her induftry, an increafe in the accu-mulations of her induftrious claffes, and a pru-dence in the economy of her individual citizens, which have raifed her to greatnefs, and fuftain her power, notwithftanding the wafte of wars, the blunders of treaties, and the tumults in peace. The people profpered at the commencement of the prefent reign. They profpered ftill more, when our colonies revolted. And this moft energetic nation continues to profper ftill.

If this marvellous profperity arifes, from the confcioufnefs of every one, that *his perfon is free* and *his property fafe*, owing to the fteady opera-tion of laws, and to the impartial adminiftration of juftice, one of the firft acts of the prefent reign muft be allowed to have given additional force to the falutary principle. A young Monarch, with

with an attachment to freedom, which merits the
commendations that pofterity will not withhold,
recommended from the throne to make the judges
commiffions lefs changeful, and their falaries more
beneficial. The Parliament feconded the zeal
of their Sovereign, in giving efficacy to a meafure, which had an immediate tendency to fecure
every right of individuals, and to give ardour to
all their purfuits. If we continue a brief review
of the laws of the prefent reign, we fhall probably find, that, whatever may have been neglected,
much has been done, for promoting the profperity and populoufnefs of this ifland.

Agriculture ought to be the great object of our
care, becaufe it is the broad foundation of every
other eftablifhment. Yet, owing in fome meafure
to the fcarcity of feafons, but much to the clamour
of the populace, we departed, at the end of the late
reign, from the fyftem which, being formed at
the Revolution, is faid to have then given ver-
dure to our fields. During every feffion, from
the demife of George II. a law was paffed for allowing the importation of falt provifions from Ireland ; for difcontinuing the duties on tallow, butter, hogs-lard, and greafe from Ireland ; till, in
the progrefs of our liberality, we made thofe regulations perpetual, which were before only temporary. We prohibited the export of grain, while
we admitted the importation of it; till, in 1773,
we fettled by a compromife, between the growers
and

and confumers, a ftandard of prices, at which both
fhould in future be free *. If by the foregoing
meafures the markets were better fupplied, the
induftrious claffes muft have been more abundantly fed: if prices were forced too low, the
farmers, and with them hufbandry, muft have both
equally fuffered. A fteady market is for the intereft of all parties, and ought therefore to be the
aim of the legiflature. On this principle the Parliament feems to have acted, when, by repealing the
laws againft engroffers, it endeavoured, in 1772, to
give a free circulation to the trade in corn. On the
other hand, various laws were paffed †, for preferving timber and underwood; for encouraging
the culture of fhrubs and trees, of roots and plants.
And additional laws were paffed for fecuring the
property of the hufbandman in the produce of his
fields, and confequently for giving force to his
diligence.

The dividing of commons, the inclofing of
waftes, the draining of marfhes, are all connected
with agriculture. Not one law, for any of thefe
valuable ends, was paffed in the warlike reign of
King William. During the hoftilities of Queen
Anne one law indeed was enacted. In the reign
of George I. feventeen laws were enacted for the
fame falutary purpofe. In the three-and-thirty
years of George II.'s reign, there were paffed a

---

* 10 Geo. III. ch. 39; 13 Geo. III. ch. 43.
† 6 Geo. III. ch. 36—48; 9 Geo. III. ch. 41.

hundred

hundred and eighty-two laws, with the fame wife
defign. Bur, during the firft fourteen feffions
of the prefent reign, no lefs than feven hundred
and two acts were obtained, for dividing of commons, inclofing of waftes, and draining of marfhes.
In this manner was more ufeful territory added
to the empire, at the expence of individuals, than
had been gained by every war fince the Revolution. In acquiring diftant dominions, through
conqueft, the ftate is enfeebled, by the charge of
their eftablifhments in peace, and by the ftill more
enormous debts, incurred in war, for their defence.
In gaining additional lands, by reclaiming the
wild, improving the barren, and appropriating the
common, you at once extend the limits of our
ifland, and make its foil more productive. Yet,
a certain clafs of writers have been ftudious to
prove, that, by making the common fields more
fruitful, the legiflature has impoverifhed the poor.

Connected with agriculture too is the making
of roads. The highways of Britain were not equal
in goodnefs to thofe of foreign countries, when the
peace of Aix-la-Chapelle was concluded. From
this epoch to the demife of George II. great exertions were certainly ufed to fupply the inconve-
nient defect. The firft fourteen feffions of the
prefent reign are diftinguifhed, not only for collecting the various road-laws into one, but for
enacting no fewer than four hundred and fifty-two
acts for repairing the highways of different diftricts. If, by this employment of many hands, nothing

thing was added to the extent of our country, every field, and every village, within it, were brought, by a more eafy conveyance, nearer to each other.

In the fame manner canals facilitate agriculture, and promote manufactures, by offering a mode of carriage at once cheaper and more certain. A very early attention had been paid to the navigation of our rivers: from *the Revolution* to the demife of George II: many ftreams had been made navigable. But, a ftill greater number have been rendered more commodious to commerce, in the prefent reign, exclufive of the yet more valuable improvement of canals. And, during the firft fourteen feffions of this reign, nineteen acts were paffed for making artificial navigations, including thofe ftupendous works, the Bridgewater, the Trent, and the Forth canals; which, by joining the Eaftern and Weftern feas, and by connecting almoft every manufacturing town with the capital, emulate the Roman labours.

In this period too, many of our harbours were enlarged, fecured, and improved: many of our cities, including the metropolis of our empire and our trade, were paved, cleanfed, and lighted. And, without including the bridges that have been built, and public edifices erected, the foregoing efforts for domeftic improvement can, with no truth, or propriety, be deemed the works of an inactive age, or of a frivolous people.

K   If

If from agriculture we turn our attention to manufactures, we shall find many laws enacted for their encouragement, some with greater efficacy and some with less. It was a wife policy to procure the *materials* of our manufactures at the cheapest rate. A tax was laid on foreign linens, in order to provide a fund, for raising hemp and flax at home; while bounties were given on these neceffary articles from our colonies, and the bounty on the exportation of hemp was withdrawn. The imposts on foreign linen yarn were withdrawn. Bounties were given on British linen cloth exported; while the making of cambricks was promoted, partly by prohibiting the foreign, and partly by giving fresh incentives, though without success, to the manufacture of cambricks within our island. Indigo, cochineal, and log-wood, the neceffaries of dyers, were allowed to be freely imported. And the duty on oak-bark imported was lowered, in order to accommodate the tanners. It is to be lamented, that the state of the public debts does not admit the abolition of every tax on materials of manufacture, of whatever country: this would be a meafure so much wifer, than giving prohibitions against foreign manufactures, which never fail to bring with them the mischiefs of monopoly; a worfe commodity, at a higher price.

The importation of filks and velvets of foreign countries was however prohibited, while the wages and combinations of filk-weavers were restrained, though

though the price of the goods was not regulated, in favour of every confumer. The workers in leather were equally favoured, by fimilar means. The plate-glafs manufacture was encouraged, by erecting a corporation for carrying it on. The making of utenfils from gold and filver was fa-voured, by appointing wardens to detect every fraud. And the law, which had been made, during the penury of King William's days, for preventing innkeepers from ufing any other plate than filver fpoons, was repealed in 1769, when we had made a very extenfive progrefs in the acquifition of wealth, and in the tafte for enjoying it.

The moft ancient ftaple of this ifland was, by prudent regulations in the fabricks of wool, fent to foreign markets, better in quality, and at a lower price.

General induftry was incited by various means, which probably had their effect. Apprentices, and workers for hire, were placed under the jurifdiction of magiftrates, who were empowered to enforce by correction the performance of contracts. Sobriety was at the fame time preferved, by reftraining the retail of fpirituous liquors. But, above all, that law muft have been attended with the moft powerful effect, which was made " for the more effectual preventing of abufes by perfons employed in the manufacture of hats, woollen, linen, fuftian, cotton, iron, leather, fur, hemp, flax, mohair, and filk; for reftraining un-

lawful

lawful combinations of every one working in such manufactures; and for the better payment of their wages." This law muft be allowed to contain the most powerful incitements of the human heart; when we confider too, that the affize of bread was at the fame time regulated.

If from a review of manufactures we infpect our fhipping, we fhall perceive regulations equally ufeful. The whale-fifheries of the river St. Lawrence and Greenland were encouraged by bounties, together with the white herring fifhery along the coafts of our ifland. Foreigners were excluded, by additional penalties, from holding fhares in Britifh fhips. And oak-timber was preferved, by new laws, for the ufe of the royal navy. The voyages of difcovery, which do fo much honour to the prefent reign, though they did not proceed from any act of the legiflature, may be regarded as highly beneficial to navigation, whether we confider the improvement of nautical fcience, or the prefervation of the mariner's health.

But, all thefe encouragements had been given in vain, had not the courfe of circulation been kept full and current, and the coin timefully reformed. New modes were prefcribed by Parliament for the recovery of fmall debts in particular diftricts. Additional remedies were adminiftered for recovering payment on bills and other mercantile fecurities in Scotland. And the iffuing of the notes of bankers was rendered more commodious and
safe.

fafe. The importation of the light filver coin of this realm was prohibited ; and what was of more importance, every tender of Britiſh filver coin, in the payment of any fum more than five-and-twenty pounds, otherwiſe than by weight, at five ſhillings and two pence per ounce, was declared unlawful. This admirable principle, fo juſt in its theory, and fo wife in its practice, was, about the fame time, applied to the gold coin. And the gold coins were recalled, and re-coined to an unexpected amount, and ordered to paſs current by weight. This meaſure, which does equal honour to the contriver, to the adviſer, and to the executor, has been attended with all the ſalutary effects, that were foretold, as to our domeſtic circulation, our foreign trade, and to our *money-exchanges* with the commercial world.

The laws, which were thus paſſed, from the acceſſion of his preſent Majeſty to the æra of the colonial revolt, had produced the moſt beneficial effects on our agriculture and manufactures, on our commerce and navigation, had not the energetic ſpirit, that actuated our affairs at the peace of 1763, continued to incite the induſtrious claſſes, and to accumulate their daily acquiſitions. If any one chooſes to appeal from general reaſonings to particular facts, let him examine the following proofs :

Years.	Ships cleared outwards.			Value of cargoes.
1764	Tons English.	D° foreign.	Total.	£.
65	639,872	68,136	708,008	14,925,950
66				

1772				
73	795,943	64,232	860,175	15,613,003
74				

Thus, our navigation had gained, in the interve-nient period, more than a hundred and fifty thou-fand tons a year, and our foreign traffic had rifen almoft a million in annual worth. The grofs re-venue of the poft-office, which, arifing from a greater or lefs correfpondence, forms, according to Anderfon, a *politico-commercial index*, amounted

in 1764 - to - £. 281,535,
in 1774* - to - 345,321.

Yet, profperous as our affairs had been, during the fhort exiftence of the peace of 1763, they were reprefented, by an analogous fpirit to that of 1738, either of defigning faction, or of unin-formed folly, as in an *alarming fituation*. The ftate of things, it was faid, is approaching to an awful crifis. The *navigation* and *commerce*, by which we rofe to power and opulence, *are much on the decline*. Our taxes are numerous and hea-vy, and provifions are dear. An enormous na-

* But the franking of letters had been now regulated, and other improvements had been meantime made.

tional

tional debt threatens the ruin of public credit. Luxury has spread its baneful influence among all ranks of people; yet, luxury is neceſſary to raiſe a revenue to ſupply the exigencies of the ſtate. Our labouring poor are forced by hard neceſſity to ſeek that comfortable ſubſiſtence in diſtant climes, which their induſtry at home cannot procure them. And the mother-country holds the rod over her children, the colonies, and, by her threatening aſpect, is likely to drive them to deſperate meaſures [*].

———————

WHEN, owing to the native habits and acquired confidence of her colonies; to the ancient neglects, and continued indulgence of Britain; to the incitements of party-men, and to the imbecility of rulers; the nation found herſelf at length obliged to enter into a ſerious conteſt with her tranſatlantic provinces, ſhe happily enjoyed all the advantages of a buſy manufacture, of a vigorous commerce, of a moſt extenſive navigation, and of a productive revenue. Of theſe animating truths we ſhall receive ſufficient conviction, by examining the following particulars:

After liquidating every claim ſubſequent to the peace of 1763, and funding every debt, by aſſigning an half-yearly intereſt for every principal,

[*] See Gent. Mag. 1774, p. 313, &c.

the

the public enjoyed an annual furplus from the public impofts of two millions two hundred thoufand
pounds, in 1764. From 1765 to 1770, this finking fund accumulated to £. 2,266,246. And from
1770 to 1775, the furplufes of all our taxes amounted annually to the vaft fum of £. 2,651,455;
which having rifen, in 1775 and 1776, to three
millions and upwards, proved a never-failing refource, amid the financial embarraffments of the
enfuing war. Thefe facts alone furnifh the moft
fatisfactory evidence of the great confumption of
the collective mafs of the people, and of their
ability to confume, from their active labours and
accumulating opulence.

Yet, during the profperous period of the peace,
there were only difcharged of the capital of the
national debt   -   -   -   £. 10,739,793.
And there remained, notwithftanding every diminution, when the war of the colonies began, in
1775   -   -   -   -   £. 135,943,051;
Whereon was paid to the public ————
creditors an annuity of   -   £. 4,440,821.*

The ftock of the Bank of England rofe mean
while from 113 *per cent.* in July, 1764, to 143
per cent. in July 1774: and difcounts on the
bills of the navy fell from 6 ⅛ *per cent.* at the firft
epoch, to 1 ¼ at the fecond. The reform of the
coin turned the nominal exchanges on the fide of

* Dr. Price, and Mr. Sinclair.

Britain,

Britain, which were in fact favourable before hoſtilities began, owing to the flouriſhing ſtate of our trade, and the advantageous courſe of our general payments. And the price of bullion fell, becauſe the ſupply was ſuperior to the demand. From the foregoing notices, an able ſtateſman might have inferred beforehand, that Great Britain never poſſeſſed ſuch reſources for a vigorous war. And this truth may be aſſerted without fear of contradiction, and without appealing to the immenſity of ſubſequent ſupplies, for unanſwerable proofs of *the fact*.

The ſurplus produce of the land and labour of England alone, which, being exported to foreign countries, might have been applied to the uſes of war, amounted to £. 15,613,003, according to an average of the years 1772—3—4 [*].

The Britiſh ſhipping, which were chiefly employed in exporting this immenſe cargo, and which were eaſily converted into tranſports, to armed ſhips, and to privateers, amounted annually to 795,943 tons: and this extenſive nurſery furniſhed the royal navy with mariners of unequalled ſkill and bravery, during a naval war, in the laſt year of which, the Parliament voted a hundred and ten thouſand ſeamen.

We may calculate from the continual progreſs in population, ariſing from additional employ-

[*] There was moreover ſent by ſea from Scotland, at the ſame time, an annual cargo of the value of £. 1,515,025, if we may believe the Cuſtom-houſe books.

ments,

ments, that there were in this ifland, at the epoch
of the colonial revolt, full 2,350,000 fighting
men.

By examining the following details, we fhall
acquire ideas fufficiently precife of the royal navy,
both before and after the war of the colonies began :—

The royal fleet carried in 1754 — 226,246 tons.
in 1760 — 300,416.
in 1774 — 276,046.

Of the king's fhips, exifting in 1774, feveral
were found, on the day of trial, unfit for actual
fervice. By an effort, however, which Britain alone
could have made, there were added to the royal
navy, during fix years of war, from 1775 to
1781 :—

	Veffels.		Guns.		Tons.
Of the line, with fifties,	44	carrying	3,002	and	56,144
Twenties to forty-fours,	110	—	3,331	—	53,350
Sloops - -	160	—	2,555	—	37,160
	314		8,888		146,654

By a fimilar effort, during fix years of the Re-
volution-war, England was only able to add to
her naval force 11,368 tons. And thus was there
a greater fleet fitted out, during the uncommon
embarraffments of the colony-war, than King
William, or Queen Anne, or even than King
George I. perhaps ever poffeffed. Of feveral of
thefe we were unhappily deprived, either by the
misfortunes incident to navigation, or by the good

2   fortune

fortune of our enemies. Yet, we had in commif-
fion, in January 1783, the fleet, whofe power will
be moft clearly perceived from the following detail *; when it is remembered, that there were
voted for the fervice of this year a hundred and
ten thoufand feamen.

Ships.		Guns.		Men.
20 of	- 80 to 108	-	carrying	15,372
44 of	- -	74	- -	26,112
45 of	- 60 to	68	- -.	24,320
18 of	- -.	50	- -	5,468
64 Frigates above 30			- -	13,765
51 Ditto under	30		- -	8,581
110 Sloops of -	18, and under,		-	11,360
15 Firefhips and bombs.				
26 Armed fhips, hired.				

393 – Navigated by - - - 104,978

Such was the naval force of Great Britain, which,
after a violent ftruggle, broke, in the end, the con-
joined fleets of France, Spain, and Holland. The
privateers of Liverpool, which have been already
ftated, alone formed a greater fleet than the armed
colonies were ever able to equip. Owing to what
fatality,

* The above ftatement, though in a different form, was
officially laid before the Houfe of Commons, at the debate on
the peace. Befides the fhips in the lift of the Navy-board,
there were feventeen, from 60 to 98 guns, ready to be com-
miffioned. Steel ftates, in his Naval Chronology, the force
of

fatality, or to what caufe, it was, that the vaft ftrength of Britain did not beat down the colonial infurgents, not in one campaign, but in three, it is the bufinefs of hiftory to explain. It may be meantime obferved, that a war carried on in *jeft*, without any *defirable* object, ought naturally to meet obftructions, and to end in difappointment.

It is now time to enquire into the loffes of our trade from the war of thofe colonies, which had been planted and nurfed with a mother's care, for the exclufive benefit of our commerce.

If it was not much interrupted by the privateers of the malcontents, we loft whole mercantile fleets to our enemies. And it muft be admitted, that in the courfe of no war, fince that of the Revolution, were our fhipping fo much deranged, or our traffic fo far driven from its ufual channels.

of the fleets of Great Britain, France, Spain, and Holland, at the end of the war, as under:

	Of the line.		Guns.
British ships - - -	145	carrying	10,132
Deduct thofe wanting repairs,	28	—	1,948
British effective - -	117	—	8,184
French - - -	82	—	5,848
Spanish - -	67	—	4,720
Dutch - - -	33	—	2,006
	182	—	12,574
Deduct thofe wanting repairs,	49	—	2,928
More than Great Britain -	16	—	1,462

But,

But, we shall see the precise state of both, by attending to the following details:

	Years.		Ships cleared outwards.			Value of cargoes.
		Tons Eng.	D° foreign.	Total.		£.
In the peaceful	1772 73 74	795,943	— 64,232	— 860,175	—	15,613,083
American war	1775 76 77	760,798	— 73,234	—. 834,032	—	13,861,812
French war —	1778	657,238	— 98,113	— 755,351	—	11,551,070
Spanish war —	1779	590,911	— 139,124	— 730,035	—	12,693,430
	1780	619,462	— 134,515	— 753,977	—	11,622,333
Dutch war —	1781	547,953	— 163,410	— 711,363	—	10,569,187
	1782	552,851	— 208,511	— 761,362	—	12,355,750

If we review this satisfactory evidence, we shall probably find, that there were annually employed, when the colony-war began, more than one hundred and fifty thousand tons of British shipping, than had been yearly employed during the prosperous years 1764—5—6; and that we annually exported of merchandizes, in the first-mentioned period more than in the last, little less than a million in value: That the colonial contest little affected our foreign commerce, if we may judge from the decreased state of our shipping *; but, if we draw our inference from the diminished value of exported cargoes, we seem to have lost £. 1,751,190 a year; which formed, probably, the real amount of the usual export to the discontented provinces: And the inconsiderable decrease in the numbers of our outward shipping, with the

* There were entered inwards of ships belonging to the revolted colonies, 34,587 tons, according to an average of the years 1771—2—3—4.

fall

fall in the value of manufactures, whereof their cargoes confifted, juftify a fhrewd remark of Mr. Eden's, " that, in the latter period, it may be doubted, whether the dexterity of exporters, which, in times of regular trade, occafions oftentatious entries, may not, in many inftances, have operated to under-valuations." It was the alarm created by the interference of France, that firft interrupted our general commerce, though our navigation and trade, in 1778, were ftill a good deal more, than the average of both, in 1755—6—7. The profperity of our foreign traffic, during the war of 1755, at leaft from the year 1758, is a fact, in our commercial annals, which has excited the a-mazement of the world. Yet, let us fairly contraft both our fhipping and our trade, great as they were affuredly, during the firft period, and little as they have been fuppofed to be, during the laft :

		Ships cleared outwards.		Value of cargoes.
Years.	Tons Eng.	D° foreign.	Total.	£.
1758	389,842	116,002	505,844	12,618,335
1778	657,238	98,113	755,351	11,551,070
1759	406,335	121,016	527,351	13,947,788
1779	590,911	139,124	730,035	12,693,430
1760	471,241	102,737	573,978	14,639,970
1780	619,462	134,515	753,977	11,622,333
1761	508,220	117,835	626,055	14,873,191
1781	547,953	163,410	711,363	10,569,187
1762	480,444	120,126	600,570	13,545,171
1782	552,851	208,511	761,362	12,355,750

What

What had occurred from the interruptions of all our foregoing wars, equally occurred from the ftill greater embarraffments of the colony-war. Temporary defalcations were, in the fame manner, faid to be infallible fymptòms of a fatal decline. In the courfe of former hoftilities, we have feen our navigation and commerce preffed down to a certain point, whence both gradually rofe, even before the return of peace removed the incumbent preffure. All this an accurate eye may perceive, amid the commercial diftreffes of the laft war. There was an evident tendency in our traffic to rife in 1779, till the Spanifh war impofed an additional burden. There was a fimilar tendency in 1780, till the Dutch war added, in 1781, no inconfiderable weight. And the year 1781, accordingly, marks the loweft degree of depreffion, both of our navigation and our commerce, during the war of our colonies. But, with the fame vigorous fpirit, they both equally rofe, in 1782, as they had rifen in former wars, to a fuperiority over our navigation and commerce, during the year, wherein hoftilities with France began.

We have beheld, too, on the return of complete peace, the fpring of our traffic rebound with mighty force. A confiderate eye may fee this in 1783 and 1784, though the burdens of war were then removed with a much more tardy hand. Twenty years before, the preliminaries of peace were fettled, in November 1762, and the definitive treaty with France and Spain was figned on

the

the tenth of February thereafter: fo that complete tranquillity was reftored early in 1763. But, owing to the greater number and variety of belligerent powers, the laft peace was fully eftablifhed by much flower fteps. The provifional articles were fettled with the feparated colonies in November 1782. The preliminaries with France and Spain were adjufted in January 1783. The definitive treaty with both, and with the United States of America, was figned on the third of September 1783. Though an armiftice was agreed on with Holland, in February 1783, preliminaries were not fettled till September thereafter, yet the definitive treaty was not figned till the twenty-fourth of May 1784. And with Tippoo Saib, who was no mean antagonift, peace was not concluded till March 1784. It was not however till July 1784, that we offered thanks to the Almighty, for reftoring to a haraffed, *though not an exhaufted nation*, the greateft bleffing, which the Almighty can beftow.

To thefe dates, and to thefe circumftances, we muft carefully attend, in forming comparative eftimates of our navigation and commerce, of the price of the public ftocks, or of the progrefs of our financial operations. With thefe recollections conftantly in our mind, we fhall be able to form fome accurate reflections, from the following details:

Epochs.	Ships cleared outwards.			Value of cargoes.
	Tons Eng.	Do foreign.	Total;	£.
1749 50 51	609,798 –	51,386 –	661,184 –	12,599,112
1764 65 66	639,872 –	68,136 –	708,008 –	14,925,950
1772 73 74	795,943 –	64,232 –	860,175 –	15,613,003
1783	795,669 –	157,969 –	953,638 –	13,851,671
84	846,355 –	113,064 –	959,419 –	14,171,375

If we examine the fubjoined ftate of the Poft-office revenue, we fhall find fupplemental proofs. The *grofs* income of *the pofts* amounted, in the year, ending the 25 March 1755, to - £. 210,663,

the 5 April 1765, to - 281,535,
the 5 April 1775, to - 345,321,
the 5 April 1784, to - 452,404.

The foregoing ftatements will furely furnifh every honeft mind with comfortable thoughts. From thefe accurate details we perceive, with fufficient conviction, how fuperior both our navigation and our commerce were, in 1783 and 1784, when peace had fcarcely returned, to the extent of both, after the treaty of Aix-la-Chapelle, an epoch of boafted profperity. We employed in our traffic, in the year 1784, THREE HUNDRED THOUSAND TONS more than we employed, according to an average of 1749—50—51, *exclufive of the fhipping of Scotland*, to no fmall amount. Of *Britifh* fhips,

L   we

we happily employed, in 1784, TWO HUNDRED
THOUSAND TONS, more than our navigation employed in 1764, though the veffels of our revolted
colonies, amounting yearly to 35,000 tons, had
been juftly excluded from our traffic, in the laft
period, but not in the firft : The value of exported
cargoes from *England* was, at both epochs, nearly
equal ; though 1784 can fcarcely be called a complete year of peace, and every induftrious people
had been admitted within the circle of a commerce,
which we had almoft ruined *the ftate*, to make
exclufively ours. The value of our exportations, in
1784, was not indeed equal to the amount of our
exports in 1764, but they were fuperior to the value of exported cargoes in 1766, 1767, and 1769 *.
If we compare 1784, when we had hardly reco-
vered from a war, avowedly carried on againft commerce, with 1774, when we had enjoyed uncommon profperity during feveral years of peace, we
fhall fee no caufe of apprehenfion, but many reafons
of hope ; the number of Britifh fhips was much
greater, in 1784, than they had been in 1774,
after we had wifely excluded the American veffels
from the protection of the Britifh flag, of which
the revolted colonifts had fhewn themfelves un-
worthy. The value of cargoes exported at both
periods are fo nearly equal, as not to merit much
confideration, far lefs to excite our fears.

Yet the government was about the fame time

* See the Chronological Table for a proof of *the fact*.

confidently

confidently told *, that unlefs the American fhipping were allowed to be our carriers, our traffic muft
ftop for want of tranfports: And the nation, for
years, had been factioufly informed, that the independence of the malecontent colonies muft prove,
at once, the deftruction of our commerce, and the
downfall of our power.

It was the prevalence of this fentiment, that
chiefly generated the colony war, fo productive of
many evils, which, like the other evils of life, have
brought with them a happy portion of good. Yet,
the fallacy of this fentiment had been previoufly
fhewn, and the effects of the abfolute independence
of our tranfatlantic provinces had been clearly
foretold. Experience has at length decided *the
fact*. For, by comparing the exports to the *difcontented colonies*, before the war began, with the exports to *the United States*, after the admiffion of
their independence, it will appear, from the following detail, that we now fupply them with manufactures to a greater amount, than even in the
moft profperous times: Thus,

		Exports.		Imports.
		£.		£.
In 1771	}			
72	}	— 3,064,843	—	1,322,532 ;
73	}			
In 1784		— 3,359,864 †	—	701,189.

Yet, the exportations of the years 1771—2—3
were beyond example great, becaufe the colonifts

* By the Committee of Weft-India Merchants, in 1783.
† From the Cuftom-houfe books.

were

were even then preparing for fubfequent events, and the exporters were induced to make their entries at the cuftom-houfe, partly by their vanity, perhaps as much by their factioufnefs. We may reafonably hope then, to hear no more of our having loft the American commerce, by the independence of the United States. From the epoch that we have met induftrious competitors in their ports, we have had too much reafon to complain of having rather traded too much with a people, who attempt to be great traders without great capitals.

Connected with the American trade is the Newfoundland fifhery. Of this Doctor Price afferts, in his ufual ftyle of depreciation and defpondence, that *we feem to have totally loft it*. The fubjoined detail, by eftablifhing fome authentic facts, will give rife, however, to more animating conclufions. Contraft the Newfoundland fifhery, as it was annually ftated, fubfequent to the peace of 1763, by Admiral Pallifer, and as it was equally reprefented, after the peace of 1783, by Admiral Campbell:

COMPARATIVE STATE *of the* NEWFOUNDLAND FISHERY.

	In 1764 - 1784 —	1765 - 1785
There were British *fifhing* fhips	141 - 236 —	177 - 292
British *trading* fhips	97 - 60 —	116 - 85
Colony fhips	205 - 50 —	104 - 58
Tonnage of British *fifhing* fhips	14,819 - 22,535 —	17,268 - 26,528
of British *trading* fhips	11,924 - 6,297 —	14,353 - 9,202
of Colony fhips	13,837 - 4,202 —	6,927 - 6,260
Quintals of fifh carried to foreign markets	470,188 - 497,884 —	493,654 - 591,276

Thus,

Thus, by excluding the fishers of the revolted colonies, we enjoy at present a more extensive fishery for the mariners of Great Britain, who, being subject to our influence, or our power, may easily be brought into action, when their efficacious aid becomes the most necessary. From those colonies a hundred and fifteen sloops and schooners used annually to bring cargoes of rum, melasses, bread, flour, and other provisions, to Newfoundland, for which the colonists were paid in bills of exchange on Britain *. To acquire this traffic for British merchants is alone a considerable advantage, which we derive from the independence of the United States. About twelve hundred sailors were accustomed to emigrate, every season, from Newfoundland to the separated colonies; where, whatever they might gain, their usefulness to Britain was lost. This drain, which is now shut up, is perhaps a still greater benefit.

Our Greenland fishery, which gives employment to so many useful people, both by land and sea, has been equally promoted by the absolute independence of the United States; as their oil and other marine productions no longer enter into competition with our own. Thus, there sailed to the Greenland seas;

* Admiral Pallifer's official report..

Years.

(150)

	Years.	Ships.	Years.	Ships,
From England in	1772 -	50 — in	1782 -	38
	1773 -	55 —	1783 -	47
	1774 -	65 —	1784 -	89
	1775 -	96 —	1785 -	140
From Scotland	-	- —	1785 -	13

——153

From this accurate detail we perceive, then, how much this important fifhery flourifhes, which had been heretofore depreffed by various competitors*.

Yet, the malecontent colonifts, who had long been the active competitors of their fellow-fubjects in Great Britain, were accuftomed to think, that this ifland could not exift without the gains of their commerce. Foreign powers equally thought, that they could ruin the affairs of Great Britain, by contributing to *their* independence. And to this fource alone may be traced up one of the chief caufes of the colony war and of the interference of foreigners. But, were we to fearch the annals of mankind, we fhould not find an example of hoftilities, which being commenced in oppofition to the genuine intereft of the belligerent parties, were continued for years in contradiction to common fenfe.

* The Britifh fifhery to Greenland has gained a manifeft fuperiority over that of the Dutch, which was once fo confiderable. In 1781 and 1782 the Dutch fent no fhips to the Greenland feas:

And in 1783 only 55 fhips.
in 1784 - 59
in 1785 - 65

The

The leaders of the malecontents feem at length
difpofed to admit, that being hurried on by paffion,
they facrificed their commerce and their happinefs to factious prejudices and to unmeaning words.
Had they been fufficiently acquainted with their
own interefts, and governed by any prudence,
they might, before the war began, have retained a
participation in Britifh privileges, and the protection of Britifh power, by verbally admitting, that
they were the fellow-fubjects of the Britifh people,
without being really incumbered with any burden.
And they might have thereby gained the prefent
independence of Ireland, with the invaluable parti-
cipations of Ireland; which, to eftimate juftly, we
ought only to fuppofe retracted for a feafon, or
even loft for a day.

It is, indeed, fortunate for us, that the French
were fo much blinded, by the fplendour of giving
independence to the Britifh colonies, as not to fee
diftinctly how much their interpofition and their aid
promoted the real advantage of Great Britain. When
the colony-war began, the true intereft of France
confifted in protracting the entanglements, which
neceffarily refulted from the virtual dependence of
thirteen diftant communities, claiming feparate
and fovereign rights; and which had continued to
enfeeble the Britifh government by their preten-
fions, their clamours, and their oppofition, till the
diffatisfied provincials had, in the fulnefs of time,
feparated themfelves, without any effort on their
part, or any ftruggle on the fide of Great Britain.
From thefe embarraffments the French have how-

ever

ever freed, by their impolicy, the rival nation. And they have even conferred on the people, whom they wished to deprefs, actual strength, by restoring, unconfcioufly, the ship-building, the freights, and the fisheries; of which the colonists had too much partaken, and which, with other facilities, have refulted to the mother country from the abfolute independence of the American states.

Spain, perhaps, as little attended to her genuine interefts, when she lent her aid to the affociated powers, which enabled the revolted colonies to take their free and equal station among the fovereign nations of the earth. She might have trufted to the hopes and fears of a British Minifter, for the fecurity of her tranfatlantic empire. But, within the American States, where can she place her truft? The citizens of thefe states have already, with their ufual enterprize, penetrated to the banks of the Miffifippi. And this active people even now bound on Louifiana and Mexico; and may even now, by intrigue, or force, shake the fidelity, or acquire the opulence, of thefe extenfive territories.

When the Dutch, by departing from their ufual caution, interpofed in the quarrel, every intelligent European perceived, that the difcontented colonies muft neceffarily be independent. And it was equally apparent, that every advantage of their traffic muft have foon been acquired, by the more induftrious nations, without the rifque of unneighbourly interference, and still more, without the charge of actual hoftilities.

When

When all parties became at length weary of a war, which had thus been carried on contrary to their genuine interefts, a peace was made. Whatever advantages of commerce, or of revenue, may have refulted from this memorable event to the other belligerent powers, certain it is, that though Great Britain contracted vaft debts, and loft many lives in the conteft, fhe derived from the independence of the American States many benefits, exclufive of *peace*, the greateft of all benefits.

Had Great Britain, like Spain, received any public revenue from her tranfatlantic territories, fhe had doubtlefs loft this income by the independence of her Colonies. If Great Britain has thereby loft fovereignty without jurifdiction, fhe has freed herfelf from the charges of protecting an extenfive coaft, without deducting any thing from her naval ftrength ; fince the colony failors were protected by pofitive ftatute * from being forced into the public fervice. While this nation has faved the annual expence of great military and civil eftablifhments, it can hardly be faid to have loft any commercial profits. And, by excluding the citizens of the United States from their accuftomed participation in the gainful bufinefs of fhip-building, freights, and fifhery, Great Britain has, in fact, made confiderable additions to her

* The 6th Anne, which had conferred the above-mentioned exemption, was indeed repealed at the commencement of the war, by the 15 Geo. III. ch. 31. § 19.

naval

naval power. Thus, the means, which were ufed
to enfeeble this country, have actually augmented
its ftrength, whatever may have been the fate of
the other belligerent parties.

It muft be admitted, however, that the Britifh
government contracted immenfe debts, by carrying on the late moft expenfive war. When thefe
were brought to account, in October 1783, the
whole debts, payable at the Exchequer, amounted
to £. 212,302,429, capital; whereon were paid
£. 8,012,061 *, as intereft and charges of management. For the payment of this annuity the
legiflature had provided funds, which, it muft be
allowed, did not produce a revenue equal to
previous expectation, or to fubfequent neceffity.
And, burdenfome as thefe debts undoubtedly were,
they had little embarraffed general circulation,
had this principal and this annuity formed the only claims on the public, owing to the Colony-
war.

But, every war leaves many unliquidated claims,
the more diftrefsful to individuals and the ftate,
as thefe unfunded debts float in the ftock-mar-
ket at great difcount; as they depreciate the value of all public fecurities; and as, from thefe
circumftances, they obftruct the financial operations of government, and prevent private perfons
from borrowing for the moft ufeful purpofes. Of
fuch unfunded debts there floated in the market,

* The Exchequer account, as publifhed by the commiffioners of public accounts.

4   in

In October 1783, no lefs than £. 18,856,542; of which £. 15,694,112 were fo far liquidated as to carry an intereft, that continually augmented the capitals, exclufive of other claims, equally cogent, but of lefs amount.

The public fecurities, which always rife in value on the return of peace, gradually fell, when thefe vaft debts were expofed to the world in exaggerated figures; when the ftockholders were terrified by declamations on the defects of their fecurity, which is, in fact, equal to the ftability of the Britifh State; and when all claimants on the public were daily affured of a truth, which had then too much exiftence, that the annual income of the public was not equal to the annual expenditure. The nation was mortified, at the fame time, by the events of a war, the mifmanagements and expences of which had made peace abfolutely neceffary. And the government was at once enfeebled, by diftractions, and unhinged, by the competitions of the great for pre-eminence and power.

It was at this crifis of unufual difficulty, that the prefent minifter was called into office, nearly as much by the fuffrages of his country, as by the appointment of his fovereign.

Were we to inftitute a comparifon of the ftate of the nation, in 1764 and 1765, with that of 1784 and 1785, we fhould be enabled to form a proper judgment, not only of the incumbrances and refources of the Britifh government, but of the meafures,

fures, which were at both periods adopted for
difcharging our debts by applying our means.
The war of 1755 augmented the public debt

$£.$ 72,111,004;

of 1775 - - - - 110,279,341.

In 1764, the *unfunded* debts, including German
claims, navy and ordnance debt, army extraor-
dinaries, deficiencies of grants and funds, exchequer bills, and a few fmaller articles, amounted to - - - - - - - - $£.$ 9,975,018;
In 1784, the *unfunded* debts, including every article of the fame
kind, amounted to - - - 24,585,157.

The navy bills fold, in 1764, at $9\frac{1}{4}$ *per cent.* difcount; in 1784, at 20 *per cent.* The value of 3
per cent. confolidated ftocks, from which the moft
accurate judgment of all ftocks may be formed,
was in 1764 at 86 *per cent.* but, in 1784, the value may be calculated at 54 *per cent.* In the firft
period, our agriculture and manufactures, our
commerce and navigation, were faid to be in the
moft profperous condition; in the laft, to be almoft undone.

With the foregoing data before us, we fhall be
able, without any minute calculations, or tedious
inquiry, to form an adequate judgment of the refources of the nation, and of the conduct of minifters, in applying thefe refources to the public
fervice, at the conclufion of our two laft wars.

11   In

In 1764—65, there were paid off and provided
   for * - - - - £. 6,192,059;
In 1784—85 - - - † 28,139,448.

There remained unprovided for

	in 1765,	—	in 1785.
German claims £.	156,044	— £.	
Navy debt -	2,426,915	—	
Exchequer bills -	1,800,000	—	4,500,000

   Total in both £. 4,382,959* — £. 4,500,000

But, let us carry this comparison one step far-
ther. There were paid off and provided for (as we
have seen) in 1764 and 65, of *unfunded* debts

         £. 6,192,159.

There were afterwards paid off before 1776 - - 10,739,793.

Total paid off in eleven years - £.16,931,952.
There were paid off and provided
   for in two years, 1784—85 - 28,139,448.

---

* Confid. on trade and finances, p. 41.
† The following are the particulars, from the annual grants
         and appropriation acts:
Debts funded in 1784, - - - £. 6,879,342.
Debts paid off and otherwise provided for, in
  1784, - - - - - 5,728,615.
Debts funded, in 1785, - - - 10,990,651.
Debts paid off and otherwise provided for, in
  1785, - - - - - 4,540,840.
Total of debts paid off, funded, and other-
  wise provided for, in 1784—85. - - } £. 28,139,448.

Yet,

Yet, from this laſt ſum muſt be deducted the £. 4,500,000 of Exchequer bills, which, being continued at the end of 1785, were either circulated by the Bank, or were in the courſe of public buſineſs lockt up in the Exchequer. Thoſe bills indeed, that paſſed into circulation, were of real uſe to the Bank, and to individuals, without depreciating funded property, as they continually paſſed from hand to hand at a premium.

There was no purpoſe, when the foregoing compariſons were inſtituted, of exalting the character of the preſent miniſter for wiſdom and energy, by the degradation of any of his predeceſſors. The able men, who managed the national finances from 1763 to 1776, acted like all former ſtateſmen, from the circumſtances wherein they were placed, and probably made as great exertions in diſcharging the national debts, as the ſpirit of the times admitted. Greater efforts have, ſince the laſt peace, been made, becauſe every wiſe man declared, that there was no effectual mode of ſecuring all that the nation holds dear, than by making the public income larger than the public expenditure. The before-mentioned operations of finance, in 1784 and 85, it had been impoſſible to perform, without impoſing many taxes, which all parties demanded as neceſſary. Were any defence required for a conduct, which, if the faithful diſcharge of duty, at no ſmall riſque of perſonal credit, is laudable, merits the greateſt praiſe, the pre-

vious

vious neceffity would furnifh ample juftifica-
tion.

What had occurred at the conclufion of every
war fince the revolution, happened in a ftill greater
degree fince the re-eftablifhment of the laft peace,
Let us make hafte to lighten the public debts,
which fo much enfeeble the ftate, and embarrafs
individuals, was the univerfal cry. It was the
judgment of the wifeft men, that, confidering the
magnitude of the national incumbrances, thefe
debts could neither be paid off, nor greatly leffened, except by a finking-fund, which fhould be in-
variably applied to this moft ufeful purpofe.
And, great as the national debts were, amounting
to £. 239,154,880 principal, which, for intereft
and charges of management, required an annuity
of £. 9,275,769, after all the financial operations of
1784 and 85, a finking-fund of a million was faid
to be fully fufficient, if thus facredly applied ; as
the productive powers of money at compound
intereft are almoft beyond calculation.

Animated by thefe reprefentations, and urged
by fenfe of duty, the minifter, though ftruggling
with the embarraffing effects of a tedious and un-
fuccefsful war, which, in the judgment of very
experienced men, had almoft exhaufted every national refource, has eftablifhed a finking-fund of a
million. Whatever might have been the univerfal
wifh, no one, at the re-eftablifhment of the peace,
had any reafonable expectation that fo large a
finking-

finking-fund would be thus early settled by act of
parliament, on principles, which at once promote
the interest of the public, by diminishing the national debt, and the advantage of individuals, by
creating a rapid circulation.

Of other finking-funds it has been remarked,
that they did not arise so much from the surpluses
of taxes, after paying the annuity, which they had
been established to pay, as from a reduction of the
stipulated interest. The finking-funds established
in Holland during 1655, and at Rome in 1685,
were thus created. The well-known finking-fund,
which had its commencement here in 1716, was
equally created by the reduction of interest on
many stocks. And hence has been inferred the
insufficiency of such funds. But, the foundation of
Mr. Pitt's finking-fund is firmly laid on a clear
surplus of a permanent revenue, made good by
new taxes, and on the constant appropriation of
such annuities as will revert to the public from the
effluxion of years.

The sufficiency and sacredness of this fund may
be however inferred, not so much from any artificial reasoning, as from the nature of the trusts,
and from the spirit of the people, which ever
guards with anxiety what has been dedicated to
their constant security and future glory. The
finking-fund of 1716 was left to the management
of ministers, who found an interest in misapplying
it. Mr. Pitt's finking-fund has been entrusted to
six commissioners, holding offices, which are no

way

way connected with each other, and to the pof-
feffors of which the people look for fidelity, knowledge, and refponfibility. From fuch truftees no
mifapplication, or jobbing, can reafonably be ap-
prehended. Add to this, that the commiffioners,
being required by law to lay out the appropriated
money in a fpecified manner, and to give an annual account of their tranfactions to Parliament,
act under the eye of a jealous world, and under
the cenfure of an independent prefs, which, in a
free country, has an efficacy beyond the penalties
of the legiflature.

But, the act itfelf, which creates this fund, and
makes thefe provifions, may be repealed, it is
feared, by the rapacity of future minifters, or by
the diftrefs of fubfequent wars.

It is however no fmall fecurity of the prefent
finking-fund, that the impolicy of mifapplying the
former is admitted with univerfal conviction and
regret. Under this public opinion, no minifter,
whatever his principles or his power may be, will
ever attempt the repeal of a law, which, in fact,
contains a virtual contract with the public creditors, and on the exiftence of which the public credit muft in future depend : For the repeal of this
act, and the feizure of this fund, during the preffures of any war, would be a manifeft breach of
this contract ; and would amount to a bankruptcy, becaufe it would be a declaration to the world,
that the nation could no longer comply with her
moft facred engagements. And what evil is to be

M   feared,

feared, or good expected, from any war, which
ought to stand in competition with the evils of
bankruptcy, or the good that must neceffarily
result from the invariable application of such a
fund ? A million, thus applied, will affuredly free
the public from vaft debts, and in no long period
yield a great public revenue: It is demonstrable,
that a finking-fund of a million, with the aid of
fuch annuities as muft meanwhile fall in, will fet free
four millions annually, at the end of twenty-feven
years: It has been demonstrated by ingenious
calculators, that the invariable application of a
million to the annual payment of debts, would,
in fixty years, difcharge £. 317,000,000 of
3 per cent. annuities, the price being at 75 per
cent. This meafure, then, is of more importance
to Great Britain than the acquifition of the American mines. And, this meafure, thus facred in its
principles and falutary in its effects, will not probably be foon repealed by any minifter, becaufe
every order in the ftate are pledged to fupport it,
while the property of every man in the community is bound for payment of the national debt.

Without inquiring minutely, whether a furplus
of £. 900,000 appeared in the exchequer on any
given day, it is fufficiently apparent, that all the
purpofes of this meafure of finance will be amply
anfwered, by the punctual payment of £. 250,000
a quarter to the truftees, as the law requires; becaufe the Parliament are engaged by the act to
make good the deficiency, if the furplus of the

10   finking-

finking-fund fhould in any year amount to lefs than
a million.

Little fluctuation in the funds will be created by
fending into the Stock Exchange a certain fum, on
certain days, during every quarter. It is the great
rife, and the proportional fall, in the value of the
ftocks, which enables jobbers to gain fortunes.
And of confequence the commiffioners will hardly
find it their intereft, if they had the inclination, to
deal in public fecurities with a view to great profits *. If the gradual and fteady rife of the ftocks
be for the intereft of the public, as well as of individuals, the quarterly application of the new
fund muft be deemed a great improvement of the
old, which was feldom felt in the ftock market,
and gave little motion to general circulation. By
thefe means will the capitals of the public debts
be rendered more manageable, in no long period;
the price of ftocks muft neceffarily rife; the finance operations of government will thereby be
performed with ftill greater advantage to the ftate;

* The purchafes being confined to the tranfer days, little
more than £. 5,000 can be brought to market on any one day,
which of confequence can make no rapid rife of any one ftock:
And, when the finking-fund amounts to the greateft poffible
fum of £. 4,000,000, the purchafe-money on any day can only
be fomething more than £. 20,000.—The gradual application
of this finking-fund is an excellent quality of it, becaufe
fudden changes in the ftock market are not for the intereft of
real buyers, or fellers. The commiffioners therefore can
gain little profit from their fuperior knowledge of the ftock
into which they intend to purchafe.

and

and induſtrious individuals will, in the ſame manner, be more eaſily accommodated with diſcounts
and loans.

The eſtabliſhment of ſuch a fund, and the creation of ſuch a truſt, are doubtleſs very important
ſervices to the people collectively, as they form a
corporation, or community. But it may be eaſily
ſhewn, that the people individually will be ſtill
greater gainers, by the new ſinking-fund, as it has
been thus judiciouſly formed. And, in this view
of the ſubject, its ſteady operation will be of ſtill
greater utility to the nation than even the payment
of debts, becauſe it is the proſperity of individuals which forms the ſtability of the ſtate. The
ingenious theoriſts, who oblige the world with
projects for paying the national debt, conſider
merely the intereſt of the corporation, or public,
without attending to what is of more real importance, the advantage of the private perſons, of
whom the public conſiſt.

A new order of buyers being thus introduced, and
a new demand thereby created, the price of ſtocks
muſt neceſſarily riſe, notwithſtanding the arts of
the ſtockjobbers ; becauſe the public ſecurities become in fact of more real value. In proportion
as the money is ſent from the ſinking-fund to the
Stock-exchange, the price of ſtocks muſt gradually
riſe ſtill higher. And a riſe of ſtocks, when gradual and ſteady, never fails to produce the moſt
ſalutary effects on univerſal circulation, by facilitating transfers of property, and by aiding the performance

formance of contracts. Recent experience confirms this general reasoning. Every one must remember how impossible it was for individuals to borrow money on any security, for any premium, till towards the end of 1784. When the stocks began to rise, the price of lands equally rose. When the government ceased to borrow, and the unfunded debts were liquidated, manufacturers and traders easily obtained discounts, and readily acquired permanent capitals.

But, the wit of man could not have devised a measure more favourable to circulation, than the sending of large sums, from day to day, into the Stock-exchange; whereby the course of circulation is constantly filled, and, being always augmented, becomes still more rapid. It is the rise of stocks, and the fulness of circulation, which make money overflow the coffers of the opulent, unless some unforeseen drain should be unhappily opened. When cash becomes thus plenty, the natural interest of money gradually falls, and bills of exchange, and other private securities, are readily discounted at a lower rate. In this happy state of things, money is said to be plenty; and every individual is accommodated with loans and with discounts, according to his needs, by pledging his property or his credit.

Owing to all these facilities, every industrious man easily finds employments. The manufacturers are all engaged. The traders send out additional adventures. The ship-owners are offered many

freights.

freights. The produce of the hufbandman is confumed by a bufy peeple. And thus are rents more
readily paid, and taxes more eafily collected.
Such are the benefits, which refult to individuals
and the ftate, from a rapid circulation, which can
only be promoted and preferved by fending money
conftantly into the Stock-exchange. It is thus,
by inciting an active induftry, that the payment of
public debts, through the channel of a quarterly
finking-fund, enables the people to pay the greateft
taxes with eafe and fatisfaction. And thus may
we folve a difficult problem in political œconomy,
whether the furplus of the public revenue ought
to be applied in the difcharge of debts, or in the
diminution of taxes : the one meafure affuredly
invigorates the induftry of the people, in the manner already defcribed ; the other may incite their
indolence, but cannot procure them an advantage
in any proportion to the benefits of unceafing employments and the accommodation of more extenfive capitals : by means of induftry the heavieft
burthens feem light : by the influence of floth the
flighteft duty appears intolerable.

It was owing, probably, to the invigorating effects of an augmented circulation, that our agriculture and manufactures, our commerce and navigation, not only flourifhed, but gradually increafed to their prefent magnitude, amidft our too
frequent wars, our additional taxes, and accumulating debts. How much the fcanty circulation of
England was filled, during the great civil wars of
the

the laſt century, by the vaſt impoſts of thoſe times, and how ſoon the intereſt of money was thereby reduced, we have already ſeen. Similar conſequences followed the wars of William and Anne, owing to ſimilar cauſes. The ſinking-fund, which for ſeveral years after its creation, in 1716, did not much exceed half a million, produced, aſſuredly, the moſt ſalutary influences, even before the year 1727: The value of the public funds roſe conſiderably, though the ſtipulated intereſt on them had been reduced, firſt, from 6 to 5 per cent. and, in that year, from 5 to 4 per cent. The natural intereſt of money gradually fell: The price of lands in the mean time advanced from 20 and 21 years purchaſe to 26 and 27: And our agriculture and manufactures, our trade and our ſhipping, kept a ſteady pace with the general proſperity of the nation *. Such are the ſalutary effects of a circulation, which, being repleniſhed by daily augmentations, is preſerved conſtantly full. And thus it is that the people are eaſed in the payment of taxes, by being better enabled to pay them, while taxes are continually augmented, though there may be particular impoſts, which ought to be repealed.

On the other hand, an obſtructed circulation never fails to create every evil which can afflict an induſtrious people: Scarcity of money, and unfavourable diſcounts; unpurchaſed manufactures, and want of employments; unpaid rents, and un-

* For the above-mentioned facts, ſee And. Chron. Com. vol. ii. p. 316—22.

M 4   performed

performed contracts; are the mischiefs, which dif-
tress every individual and embarrass the community, while circulation is impeded. The commerce of England was well nigh ruined, during
King William's reign, by the diforders in the
coin, the want of confidence, and the high price of
money. The foreign bankruptcies, in 1764, reduced the value of cargoes, which were exported in
this year, from fixteen millions to fourteen, during
feveral years, owing to the decline of general credit. How much the domeftic bufinefs of Great
Britain was affected by the home bankruptcies of
1772 *, is ftill remembered. The complaints,
which were at thofe periods made of a decline of
commerce, were alone owing to an obftructed circulation, as fubfequent experience hath amply
evinced.

Wars, then, in modern times, are chiefly deftructive, as they incommode the induftrious claffes, by obftructing circulation. Yet, general induftry was not much retarded, however individual
perfons, or particular communities, may have been

* The following detail is alone fufficient to demonftrate
how the manufactures of a country may be ruined by a lan-
guid circulation. Of linen cloth there were ftamped for fale
in Scotland,

during 1771 — 13,466,274 yards.
    1772 — 13,089,006.
    1773 — 10,748,110.
    1774 — 11,423,115.

deranged,

deranged, or injured, by the colony war. The
people were able to confume abundantly, since
they actually paid vaft contributions, by their daily confumption of excifeable commodities*. And
though they purfued their accuftomed occupations,
and thus paid vaft impofts, the eftablifhed income
of the ftate fuftained confiderable defalcations
from various caufes; from the abufes, which war
never fails to introduce into certain branches of the
revenue; from the illicit traffic, that generally
prevails in the courfe of hoftilities; and from the
new impofitions, which fomewhat leffen the ufual
produce of the old.

These diforders in the public revenue have been
at leaft palliated, if they have not been altogether cured, fince the re-eftablifhment of peace.
The meafures, which were vigoroufly adopted, for
the effectual prevention of fmuggling; the altera-
tions, which have been made in the collection of

* Of malt there were confumed,

	Bufh.	Old Duties.
in 1773—4—5	72,588,010	£. 1,814,700.
in 1780—1—2	87,343,083	2,183,577.

Of low wines from corn,

	Gal.	Old Duties.
in 1773—4—5	9,974,837	£. 415,593.
in 1780—1—2	11,757,499	489,895.

Of Soap,

	lb.	Old Duties.
in 1773—4—5	93,190,140	£. 582,438.
in 1780—1—2	98,076,806	612,980.

fome

fome departments of the public income; and the improvement.that has been happily effected in all; have brought and continue to bring vaft fums into the Exchequer *. The public expenditure continually diftributes this vaft revenue among the creditors, or fervants of the State, who return it to the original contributors, either for the neceffaries, or the luxuries of life. The Exchequer, which thus conftantly receives and difpenfes this immenfe income, has been aptly compared to the human heart, that unceafingly carries on the vital circulation, fo invigorating while it flows, fo fatal when it ftops. Thus it is, that modern taxes, which are never hoarded but always expended, may even promote the employments and induftry, the profperity and populoufnefs, of an induftrious people.

The conteft, which had been carried on during the war of 1755, between Doctor Brackenridge and Doctor Forfter, with regard to the effects of our policy, both in war and peace, on population, was revived amidft our Colony contefts by Dr. Price and his opponents. By taking a wider range, and eftablifhing many new facts, this laft

* The whole public revenue paid into the Exchequer,

from Michaelmas 1783 } —£. 12,995,519.
to   ditto   1784 }

Ditto, from Michaelmas 1784 } —— 15,379,182.
to   ditto   1785 }

Ditto, from 5 January 1785 } —— 15,397,471.
to   ditto   1786 }

controverfy

controverfy furnifhes much more inftruction, on
a, very interefting fubject, than the laft. Doctor
Price revived the difpute, by contributing an Appendix to Mr. Morgan's Effay on Annuities,
wherein the Doctor attempts to prove, by ingenious remarks on births and burials, a gradual decline in the populoufnefs of Great Britain. He
was foon encountered by Mr. Arthur Young, who
juftly inferred, from the progrefs of improvements
in agriculture, in manufactures, in commerce, an
augmentation in the number of people. Mr.
Eden publifhed, in 1779, elegant criticifms * on
Doctor Price; by which he endeavours to inva-
lidate the argument, drawn from a comparifon of
the number of houfes at the Revolution, and at
prefent; infifting that the firft muft have been lefs,
and the laft much greater, than the text had allowed. The Doctor fhewed fome miftakes in his antagonift, without adding much to the force of his
own argument by his reply. Yet, if we may credit his coadjutor, *he confidered his fyftem as more
firmly eftablifhed than ever* †.

This long-continued controverfy now found
other fupporters. Mr. Wales publifhed his Accurate Inquiry in 1781. With confiderable fuccefs
he overthrows Doctor Price's fundamental argument, from the comparifon of houfes at different periods; by fhewing, that the returns of houfes to the

---

* In his Letters to Lord Carlifle.
‡ Uncertainty of Population, p. 9.

tax-

tax-office are not always precife ; by proving, from actual enumerations of feveral towns at diftant periods, that they had certainly increafed ; by evincing, from the augmented number of births, that there muft be a greater number of breeders. This able performance was immediately followed by Mr. Howlet's ftill more extenfive examination of Doctor Price's effay. Mr. Howlet expands the arguments of Mr. Wales ; he adds fome illuftrations ; and, what is of ftill greater importance, in every inquiry, he eftablifhes many additional facts.

The treatifes of Meff. Wales and Howlet made a great impreffion on the public. At the moment, when they had gained—*a confiderable fhare of popular belief*, it was deemed prudent on the fide of Doctor Price to publifh—*Uncertainty of the prefent population*. This writer frankly declares that *he is convinced by neither party*, and that he muft confequently remain *in a ftate of doubt and fceptical fufpenfe*. His apparent purpofe is to fhew, in oppofition to *the popular belief*, that after all our refearches, *we really know nothing with any certainty*, as to this important part of our political œconomy. In the fceptical arithmetic of this dubious computer, 1,300,000, multiplied by 5, produce 6,250,000. Doctor Price and his coadjutors feemed unwilling to admit, that if there were, in England and Wales, at Lady day 1690, 1,300,000 *inhabited houfes*, and *five perfons* in each, there muft neceffarily have been, at the fame time, 6,500,000 fouls. For, they feared the charge of abfurdity,

in

in fuppoſing a decreaſe of *a million and a half of people*, during ninety years of *augmented employments*: And, they perceived, that by admitting there were in 1690, ſix million and a half of people, they would thereby be obliged to admit, that there had been an augmentation of a million and a half, during the foregoing century, notwithſtanding the long civil wars, and the vaſt emigrations. The Doctor publiſhed, in 1783, Remarks on theſe tracts of Meſſ. Wales and Howlet *. And, with his uſual acuteneſs, he detects ſome miſtakes ; but, with his accuſtomed pertinacity, he adheres to his former opinions.

The matter in diſpute, we are told †, muſt be determined, not by vague declamation, or ſpeculative argument, but by well-authenticated facts : For, " the grand argument of Dr. Price is at once extremely clear, and comprehended in a very narrow compaſs." The following is the ſtate, of this *grand argument* :

That there appeared by the Hearth-books, at Lady day 1690, to be in England and Wales - - - - 1,300,000 ;

That there appeared by the Tax-office books, in 1777, only - 952,734:

Whence, the Doctor inferred, as a neceſſary conſequence, that there had been a proportional diminution of people, ſince 1690.

* In his Obſervations on Reverſionary Payments, in 2 vol. 8vo.
† By *Uncertainty of Population.*

5   Conſidering

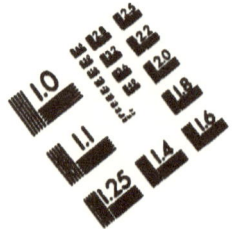
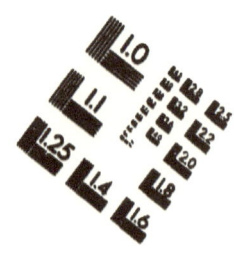

**IMAGE EVALUATION
TEST TARGET (MT-3)**

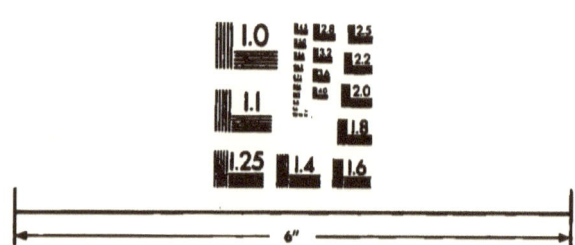

6"

Photographic
Sciences
Corporation

25 WEST MAIN STREET
WEBSTER, N.Y. 14580
(716) 872-4503

Confidering how important this subject is to the state, and how much it is connected with the general purpose of this Estimate, I was led to examine, at once with minuteness and with brevity, an argument, which has been oftentatiously displayed as equal in its inferences to the certainty of actual enumerations.

In lieu of the obnoxious hearth-tax, the Parliament impofed, in 1696, a duty of two fhillings on every houfe; fix fhillings on every houfe containing ten windows, and fewer than twenty; and ten fhillings on every houfe having more than twenty windows; thofe *occupiers* only excepted, who were exempted from church and poor rates. And Gregory King computed, with his ufual precifion, what the tax would produce, before it had yielded a penny *. Thus, fays he, the number of *inhabited houfes* is — — — — — 1,300,000;

whereof, under 10 windows 980,000.

under 20 windows 270,000.

above 20 windows 50,000.
——————
1,300,000.

Out of which deducting,

for thofe receiving alms	— — — — 330,000 houfes at 2s.	£. 33,000.
for thofe not paying to church and poor 380,000	at 2s. 4d.	44,000.
for omiffions, frauds, and defaulters	40,000 — — at 4s.	8,000.
	———————	———————
Infolvent	750,000.	£. 85,000.
Solvent	550,000; Paying but	119,000.

However many *infolvent* houfes were thus deducted from the 1,300,000 *inhabited houfes*, Gregory

* Pol. Obferv. Brit. Muf. Harl. MSS. 1898.

King

King allowed at laft too many *folvent* ones. This truth may be inferred from the following *fact.* There remains in the tax-office * a particular account of the money, which each county paid in 1701, for the before-mentioned tax of 1696, from the affeffments of Lady-day 1700, and which amounted to £. 115,660

But, the oldeft lift of houfes, which fpecifically paid the tax of 1696, is " *an account made up, for 1708, from an old furvey book,*" but from *prior* affeffments : And this account ftands thus :

Houfes at 2s. — 248,784, produced £. 24,878.
6s. — 165,856, ——————— 49,757.
10s. — 93,876, ——————— 46,398.

508,516, producing £.121,573.

He who does not fee a marvellous coincidence †, between this official document and the previous calculation of Gregory King, muft be blind indeed. The *folvent* houfes of King, and the *charged* houfes of 1708, are of the fame kind, both being thofe houfes which *actually paid*, or were fuppofed to have paid,

* I have ranfacked the tax-office for information on this litigated but important fubject; and I was affifted in my refearches by the intelligent officers of this department, with an alacrity, which fhewed, that, having fully performed their duty to the public, they did not fear minute infpection.

† The houfes having *upwards* of twenty windows, in the tax-office account of 1781, are 52,373. The number of the fame kind allowed by King is 50,000 : But he is not fo fortunate in his other calculations.

the

the tax. And, Mr. Henry Reid, a comptroller of the tax-office, noted for his minute diligence and attentive accuracy, reported to the Treasury, in October 1764, that the old duties, on an average, produced yearly, from 1696 to 1709 — £. 118,389*.

But, there must have necessarily been a great many more houses, in 1708, than the 908,516, charged, and paying £. 121,579. In the twelve years from 1696, there could have been no great waste of houses, however powerful the destructive cause might have been. And Gregory King, in order to make up his thirteen hundred thousand houses, calculated the *dwellings* of *the poor*, in 1696,

at - - - - - 710,000;
and of defaulters, &c. at - - 40,000;
                              ————
                              750,000.

Davenant † stated, in 1695, from the hearth-books, the cottages, *inhabited by the poorer sort*, at 500,000; and he afterwards asserts, as Doctor Price observes, that there were in 1689, houses, called cottages, having one hearth, to the number of 554,631: whence we may equally suppose, that there were dwellings, having two hearths, a very considerable number, whose inhabitants, either receiving alms, or paying none, did not contribute to the tax of 1696: so that, in 1708, there must have certainly existed 710,000 dwellings of the poor; as this number had certainly existed in 1696.

* Gregory King calculated the tax beforehand at £.119,000.
† Vol. i. edit. 1st, p. 5.

Mr.

Mr. Henry Reid moreover reported to the Treasury, in 1754, that in the year 1710, when an additional duty took place, it became an universal practice to stop up lights; so that, in 1710, the old duties yielded only £. 116,676: —And, for some years, both the old and the new duty suffered much from this cause, as there was no penalty for the stopping of windows. Other duties, continues he, were imposed in 1747 *; so that from Lady-day 1747, to Lady-day 1748, the whole duties yielded £. 208,093 : and, an explanatory act having passed in 1748, the duties yielded, for the year ending at Lady-day 1749, £. 220,890 : But, other modes of evading the law being soon found, the duties decreased year after year.—And thus much from the intelligent Mr. Henry Reid, who never dreamed of houses falling into non-existence.

The first account of houses, which now appears to have been made up, subsequent to that of 1708, is the account of 1750, and the last is that of 1781. With the foregoing data before us, we

* By 20 Geo. II. ch. 3 : which recites, that whereas it hath often been found from experience, that the duties granted by former acts of parliament have been greatly lessened by means of persons frequently stopping up windows in their dwelling houses, in order to evade payment; and it hath often happened, that several assessments have not been made in due time; and that persons remove to other parishes without paying the duty for the houses so quitted, to the prejudice of the Revenue. But the legislature do not recite, that houses daily fell down, or that the numbers of the people yearly declined.

may

may now form a judgment sufficiently precise, in respect to the progress of our houses, *charged* and *chargeable* with the house and window tax.

The charged, in 1696, according to King, 550,000
The chargeable, *according to him*, - 40,000
                                              ─────────
                                              590,000

The charged and chargeable, in 1750, 729,048 *

    Increase in 54 years   -   -   139,048

The charged, in 1708,   -   -   -   508,516
The chargeable, let us suppose,   -   100,000
                                              ─────────
                                              608,516

The charged and chargeable, in 1781, 721,351

    Increase in 73 years .   .   -   112,835.
                                              ─────────

Here then is a solution of the difficult problem, in political œconomy, which has engaged so many able pens, Whether there exist as many houses, at present, as there certainly were, in England and Wales, at the Revolution ; at least, the question is decided, as to the number of houses, *charged* and *chargeable* with the window and house tax : And of consequence the middling and higher ranks of men must, with the number of their dwellings, have necessarily increased.

* This high number, in 1750, was probably owing to the act of parliament, 20 Geo. II, which had just past, when new modes of circumvention had not yet taken place.

A great

A great difficulty, it muft be admitted, ftill remains, which cannot be altogether removed, though many obftructions may be cleared away. The difficulty confifts, in afcertaining, with equal precifion, the number of dwellings, which have been exempted, by law, from every tax fince 1690, on account of the occupiers poverty. The litigated point muft at laft be determined by an anfwer to the queftion, Whether the lower orders are more numerous in the prefent day than in the former.

A modern fociety has been compared, with equal elegance and truth, to a pyramid, having the higher ranks for its point, and the lower orders for its bafe. Gregory King left us an account of the people, minutely divided into their feveral claffes, which, though formed for a different purpofe, contains fufficient accuracy for the prefent argument *.

* Davenant's works.

RANKS.

RANKS.	Number of Families.	Heads in each.	Number of Persons.
Peers	186	30	6,920
Knights	660	13	7,800
Baronets	800	16	12,800
Eminent clergymen	2,000	6	12,000
Eminent merchants	2,000	8	16,000
Esquires	3,000	10	30,000
Military officers	4,000	4	16,000
Naval officers	5,000	4	20,000
Persons in lesser offices	5,000	6	30,000
Persons in higher offices	5,000	8	40,000
Lesser clergymen	8,000	5	40,000
Lesser merchants	8,000	6	48,000
Persons in the law	10,000	7	70,000
Persons of the liberal arts	15,000	5	75,000
Freeholders of the better sort	40,000	7	280,000
Shopkeepers and tradesmen	50,000	4½	225,000
Artizans	60,000	4	240,000
Freeholders of the lesser sort	120,000	5½	660,000
Farmers	150,000	5	750,000
Common soldiers	35,000	2	70,000
Common sailors	50,000	3	150,000
Labourers and out-servants	364,000	3½	1,275,000
Cottagers, paupers, and vagrants	400,000	3½	1,330,000
			5,550,520

If

If this division of the people should be deemed only probable, it would prove, with sufficient conviction, how many dwellings the two last classes required to shelter them, since they contained no fewer than *two million six hundred and five thousand persons*. Gregory King allotted for them, as we have seen, 550,000 houses. And it is apparent, that if the two lower orders of men have augmented, with the progress, which has been traced in our agriculture and manufactures, in our traffic and navigation, they must necessarily dwell in additional houses.

Davenant has shewn, that the poor-rates of England and Wales amounted, towards the end of Charles II.'s reign, to - - £. 665,302. By an account given in to parliament,

in 1776, the poor-rates amounted to 1,556,804.

However this vast sum, which is probably under the truth, may have been misapplied, or wasted, yet every one who received his proportion of it, as alms, was exempted from the tax on chargeable houses, and must have consequently swelled the number of cottages.

Whatever the term *cottage* may have signified formerly, it was described, by the statute of the 20 Geo. II. as a house, having nine windows, or under, whose inhabitant either receives alms, or does not pay to church and poor. But, we are not inquiring about *the word*, but *the thing*; whether the *dwellings* of the lower orders, of whatever denomination, have increased, or diminished, since

N 3   the

the Revolution; and the end of this inquiry is to find, whether the lower orders of men have decreased or augmented.

The argument for a decreased number of cottages is this: Gregory King, from a view of the hearth-books of 1690, (which yet did not contain the cottages, since they were not chargeable with the hearth-tax) calculated the dwellings of those, who either received alms, or did not give any, at - - - - - 550,000.
The surveyors of houses returned the

number of cottages, in 1759 *, at - 282,429;
and in 1781 - - 284,459.

Forster, the antagonist of Brackenridge, was the first, probably, who objected to the accuracy of the surveyors returns, with regard to *all* houses. Having obtained the *collectors rolls*, he had *counted*, in 1757, the number of houses in nine contiguous parishes; whereby he found, that, out of 588 houses, only 177 paid the tax; that Lambourn parish, wherein there is a market-town, contains 445 houses, of which 229 only pay the tax. When it was objected to Forster, that this survey was too narrow for a general average, he added afterwards nine other parishes, in distant counties;

---

* This is the first year, says Doctor Price, that an order was given to return the cottages excused for poverty. I have in my possession some returns which were made of cottages in 1757, and which, having escaped the destruction of time, evince previous orders and previous performance. There was, in fact, an account of the cottages made up at the tax-office in 1756.

2   whereby

whereby it appeared, that of 1,049 houses, only 349 were charged with the duty; whence he inferred, that the *cottages* are to the *taxable houses* as more than *two* to *one*.* Mr. Wales equally objected to the truth of the surveyors returns, in their full extent. And Mr. Howlet endeavoured, with no small success, to calculate the average of their errors, in order to evince what ought probably to have been the true amount of the genuine numbers. * In this calculation, Doctor Price hath doubtless shewn petty faults; yet is there sufficient reason to conclude, with Doctor Forster and Mr. Howlet, that the houses returned to the tax-office are to the whole, as 17 are to 29, nearly. It will at last be found, that the returns of taxable houses are very near the truth; but that the reports of exempted houses cannot possibly be true: for 280,000, or even 300,000 cottages, would not contain the two lower orders who existed in England and Wales at the Revolution; and who, with the greatest aid of machinery, could not perform the annual labour of the same countries at present.

Our agriculture has at all times employed the greatest number of hands, because it forms the support of our manufactures, our traffic, and our navigation. It admits of little dispute, whether our

* Forster's letter, in December 1760, which the Royal Society declined to publish. [MSS. Birch, Brit. Muf. No. 4440.] The algebraical sophisms of Brackenridge were printed in the foreign gazettes: the true philosophy of Forster, by *experiment* and *fact*, was buried in the rubbish of the Royal Society.

husbandry

husbandry has been purfued, before or fince the
bounty on the export of corn, in 1689, with the
greateft fkill, diligence, and fuccefs. Mr. Arthur
Young found, in 1770, by inquiries in the counties, and by calculations from minutes of fufficient
accuracy, that the perfons engaged in farming
alone amounted to 2,800,000 ; befides a vaft
number of people, who are as much maintained by
agriculture as the ploughman that tills the foil [*].
Yet, the two lower ranks of Gregory King, including the labouring people and out-fervants, the
cottagers, paupers, and vagrants, amounted only
to 2,600,000.

Of the general ftate of our manufactures at the
Revolution, and at prefent, no comparifon can
furely be made, as to the extenfivenefs of their
annual value, or to the numerofity of ufeful people employed by them. The woollen manufacture
of Yorkfhire alone is in the prefent day of equal
extent with the woollen manufactures of England
at the Revolution. By an account, formed at the
aulnager's office, it appears, that the woollen goods
exported in 1688, were valued at two millions,
exclufive of the home confumption, of much lefs
amount [†]. The manufacturers furnifhed the committee of privy council, on the Irifh arrangements,
with " a particular eftimate of the Yorkfhire woollen manufactures ;" whereby it appeared, that
there were exported yearly of the value of

[*] North, Tour, vol. iv. p. 364—5.
[†] MSS, Harl. Brit. Muf. N° 1898, for a minute account.

£. 2,371,942,

£. 2,371,942, and confumed at home £. 901,759*. We know, with fufficient certainty, from the cuftom-houfe books, that after clothing the inhabitants, there were exported of the value of woollens, according to an average of the years 1699—1700—1, the value of - - £. 2,561,615 : from average of 1769—70—71 - 4,323,463.

And this manufacture, which has been always regarded as the greateft, continues to flourifh, and to employ, as it is faid, a million and a half of people.

Since the epoch of the Revolution, we may be faid to have gained the manufactures of filks, of linen, of cotton, of paper, of iron, and the potteries, with glafs, befides other ingenious fabrics; which all employ a very numerous and ufeful race. We may indeed determine, with regard to the augmentation of our manufactures, and to the increafe of our artizans, from the following detail:

There were exported, according to an average of the years 1699—1700—1701, products, *exclufive of the woollens before mentioned*, of the value of - - - £. 3,863,810. Ditto in 176 —70—71 - - 10,565,196.

Thus have we demonftration, that while our woollen manufactories nearly doubled in their extent, during feventy years, our other manufactures had more than trebled in theirs. And therefore it is equally demonftrable, that the great body of artifts,

* The Council Report.

how

who were conftantly employed in all thefe manufactories, muft have increafed nearly in the fame
proportion, during the fame bufy period.

The whole failors, who were found in England,
   by enumeration, in January 1700—1, amounted
   to -   -   -   - *16,591.

By a calculation, which agreed nearly
   with the accuracy of this enumeration,
   there appeared to have been annually
   employed in *the merchants fervice*, between the years 1764 and 74   -   59,565.

The tonnage of Englifh fhipping
   during King William's reign, a-
   mounted only to   -   - 230,441 tons.
D° during the prefent reign - 992,754

We may thence certainly determine, with regard
to the number of ufeful artificers, who muft have
been employed during the latter period more than
in the former, in building and repairing our fhips.
It is hufbandry, then, and manufactures, commerce, and navigation, which every where, in later
ages, employ and maintain the great body of the
people. Now, the labour demanded during the
prefent reign, to carry forward the national bufinefs, agricultural and commercial, could not by
any poffibility have been performed by the inferior numbers of the induftrious claffes, who doubtlefs exifted in the reign of King William. And

* There is reafon to believe, however, that the above enumeration did not contain the failors of the port of London.

from

from the foregoing reasonings and facts, we may
certainly conclude, with one of the ableft writers
of any age on political œconomy : " The liberal
reward of labour, as it is the effect of increafing
wealth, fo it is the caufe of increafing population :
To complain of it [high wages] is to lament over
the necessary effect and caufe of the greateft public
profperity *.

In calculating the numbers of people, we muft
attentively confider the ftate of fociety in which
they exift ; whether as fifhers and hunters, as
fhepherds and hufbandmen, as manufacturers and
traders ; or as in a mixed condition, compofed
partly of each. The American tribes, who reprefent the firft, are found to be inconfiderable in
numbers ; becaufe they do not eafily procure fubfiftence from their vaft lakes and unbounded fo-
refts, by fifhing and hunting. The Afiatic Tar-
tars, who reprefent the fecond ftage of fociety, are
much more populous ; fince they derive continual plenty from their multitudinous flocks. But,
even thefe are by no means equal in population
to the Chinefe, who acquire their comforts from
an unremitting induftry, which they employ in
agriculture, in manufacture, in the arts, in fifheries,
though not in navigation. It was foreign commerce which peopled the marfhes of the Adriatic

* See the Inquiry into the Caufes of the Wealth of Nations, ch. 8 ; wherein Dr. Adam Smith treats *Of the Wages of
Labour*, and incidentally of population, with a perfpicuity,
an elegance, and a force, which have been feldom equalled.

and

and the Baltic, during the middle ages; hence
arose Venice and the Hanfe towns, with their envied opulence and naval power. It was the conjunction of agriculture, manufactures, and traffic,
which filled *the Low Countries* with populous
towns, with unexampled wealth, and with marvellous energy. The fame caufes that produced all
thofe effects, which hiftory records, as to induftry,
riches, and ftrength, continue to produce fimilar
effects at prefent.

When England was a country of fhepherds and
warriors, we have beheld her inconfiderable in
numbers. When manufacturers found their way
into the country, when hufbandmen gradually
acquired greater fkill, and when the fpirit of commerce at length actuated all; people, we have
feen, grow out of the earth, amidft convulfions,
famine, and warfare. He who compares the population of England and Wales at the Conqueft,
at the demife of Edward III. at the year 1588,
with our population in 1688, muft trace a vaft
progrefs in the intervenient centuries. But England can fcarcely be regarded as a manufacturing
and commercial country at the Revolution, at
leaft when contrafted with her prefent profperity.
The theorift, then, who infifts, that our numbers have
thinned, as our employments have increafed, and
our population declined, as our agriculture and
manufactures, our commerce and navigation, advanced, argues againft facts, experience, and even
againft daily obfervation.

Yet,

Yet, Doctor Price and his followers contend, that our induſtrious claſſes have dwindled the moſt ſince 1749, becauſe it is from this epoch that the proſperity of the people has been the greateſt, however they may have, at any time, been governed. And the following argument is ſaid to amount to demonſtration, becauſe *it contains as ſtrong a proof of progreſſive depopulation as actual ſurveys can give* * : The number of houſes returned to the tax-office, as *charged* and *chargeable*, was, — in 1750 — 729,048

in 1756 — 715,702

in 1759 — 704,053

in 1761 — 704,543

in 1777 — 703,473

For a moment Doctor Price would not liſten to the ſuggeſtion, that the houſes may have *exiſted*, though they were not *included* in the returns of the intermediate years. But, lo! additional returns have been made up at the tax-office, amounting, in 1781 to 721,351.

---

* Dr. Price's Eſſay on Popul. p. 38.

As

As a fupplemental proof*, which may give fatif-
faction to well-meaning minds, there is annexed
*a comparative view of the number of houfes in each
county, as they appeared to Davenant, in the hearth-
books of 1690; of the charged houfes in 1708, with
the duties actually paid by them; of the chargeable
houfes in 1750; with the houfes of the fame defcription,
in 1781.*

* The chargeable houfes,
    in 1781, *under* 10 windows, are — 497,801
             under 21 windows, — — 171,177
             above 20 windows, — — 52,373
                                         ——————
                                         721,351
    Cottages - - - - 284,459

    Total houfes and cottages, in 1781, 1,005,810
    The houfes in 1750 — 729,048
    The cottages in 1756 — 274,755
                                         ——————
                                         1,003,803

    Increafe fince 1750 — — 2,007

The account of cottages, in 1756, was completed, as appears
from the tax-office books, on the 20th of November 1756. And
thus, by adopting the mode and the materials of Doctor Price's
argument, it is fhewn, that he has been extremely miftaken,
as to the depopulation of England, fince 1750.

A COM-

A COMPA[
England
1690, an
1781.

COUNTIE[

Bedfordfhire
Berks - -
Bucks -
Cambridge
Chefter -
Cornwall -
Cumberland
Derby - -
Devon -
Dorfet -
Durham -
York - -
Effex - -
Gloucefter
Hereford -
Hertford -
Huntingdon
Kent - -
Lancafhire
Leicefter -
Lincoln -
London, &c.
Norfolk -
Northampton
Northumberla
Nottingham
Oxford -
Rutland -
Salop - -
Somerfet -
Southampton,
Stafford -
Suffolk -
Surrey, &c.
Suffex - -
Warwick -
Weftmorland
Wilts - -
Worcefter
Anglefea
Brecon -
Cardigan -
Carmarthen
Carnarvon
Denbigh -
Flint - -
Glamorgan
Merioneth
Monmouth
Montgomery
Pembroke
Radnor -

A COMPARATIVE VIEW of the Number of HOUSES, in each County of England and Wales, as they appeared in the Hearth-books of Lady-Day 1690, and as they were made up at the Tax-office in 1708—1750—and in 1781.

COUNTIES.	No of Houses, 1690.	No of Houses charged, 1708.	Money paid, by the charged Houses, 1708.	No of Houses, charged and chargeable, 1750.	No of Houses, charged and chargeable, 1781.
Bedfordshire - -	12.170	5,479	£.1,315 14	6,802	5,360
Berks - - -	16,966	7,558	2,211 4	9,762	8,277
Bucks - - -	18,688	8,604	2,216 8	10,687	8,670
Cambridge - -	18,619	7,220	1,635 16	9,334	9,088
Chester - -	25,592	11,656	2,682 0	16,006	17,201
Cornwall - -	21,613	9,052	1,649 0	14,520	15,274
Cumberland - -	15,279	2,509	513 18	11,914	13,419
Derby - - -	24,944	8,260	1,669 4	13,912	14,046
Devon - - -	56,202	16,686	3,420 8	30,049	28,612
Dorset - - -	17,859	4,113	980 6	11,711	11,132
Durham - -	53.345	6,298	1,114 4	10,475	12,418
York - -	121,051	44,779	7,788 14	70 816	76,224
Essex - - -	40,545	16,250	5,046 4	19,057	18,389
Gloucester - -	34,476	13,285	3,721 14	16,251	14,950
Hereford - -	16,744	6,913	1,546 10	8,771	8,092
Hertford - -	17,488	7,447	2,132 2	9,251	8,618
Huntingdon - -	8,713	3,994	859 0	4,363	3,847
Kent - - -	46,674	21,871	5,883 2	30,029	30,975
Lancashire - -	46,961	22,588	4,332 12	33,273	30,956
Leicester - -	20,448	8,584	1,889 4	12,957	12,545
Lincoln - -	45,019	17,571	3,392 2	24,999	24,591
London, &c. -	111,215	47,031	16,210 14	71,977	74,704
Norfolk - -	56,579	12,097	3,495 14	20,697	20,056
Northampton -	26,904	9,218	2,216 4	12,464	10,350
Northumberland { included in Durham.		6,787	979 18	10,453	12,431
Nottingham - -	17,818	7,755	1,528 6	11,001	10,872
Oxford - - -	19,627	8,502	2,278 12	10,362	8,693
Rutland - - -	3,661	1,498	310 8	1,873	1,445
Salop - - -	27,471	11,452	2,358 8	13,332	12,895
Somerset - -	45,900	19,043	4,613 18	27,822	26,407
Southampton, &c.	28,557	14,331	3,585 18	18,045	15,828
Stafford - -	26,278	10,818	2,372 8	15,917	16,483
Suffolk - -	47,517	15,301	4,970 14	18,834	19,589
Surrey, &c. -	40,610	14,071	3,972 18	20,037	19,381
Sussex - - -	23,451	9,429	2,898 18	11,170	10,574
Warwick - -	22,400	9,461	2,440 10	12,759	13,276
Westmorland -	6,691	1,904	349 12	4,937	6,144
Wilts - - -	27,418	11,373	2,959 10	14,303	12,856
Worcester - -	24,440	9,178	2,519 8	9,967	8,791
Anglesea - -		1,040	147 8	1,334	2 204
Brecon - -		3,370	478 8	3,234	3,407
Cardigan - -		2,042	237 12	2,542	2,444
Carmarthen - -		3,985	475 2	5,020	5,126
Carnarvon - -		1,583	211 18	2,366	2,675
Denbigh - -		4,753	709 18	6,091	5,678
Flint - - -		2,653	400 10	3,520	2,990
Glamorgan - -		5,020	707 12	6,290	5,146
Merioneth - -		1,900	246 12	2,664	2,972
Monmouth - -		3,289	731 14	4,930	4,454
Montgomery - -		4,047	588 6	4,890	5,421
Pembroke - -		2,764	347 12	3,803	3,224
Radnor - - -	77,921	2,092	327 8	2,425	2,076
	1,319,215	508,516	£·121,573 4	729,048	721,351

(Welsh counties from Anglesea to Radnor are bracketed under "South and North Wales.")

From this inſtructive document it appears, that
twenty counties, including London, Weſtminſter,
and Middleſex, have actually increaſed, ſince 1750.
But it is an abuſe of words to ſpeak of houſes
having actually increaſed: the proper language is,
that in twenty counties the ſurveyors have been
more diligent, and made more accurate returns,
than in other diſtricts. Let us take the example
of Surrey and Lancaſhire, which are ſtated, as having decreaſed in houſes, and conſequently in people, ſince 1750 *. It is apparent, that Surrey has
been overflowed by London, during the laſt five-
and-thirty years †. And of Lancaſhire, conſidering the vaſt augmentations of its domeſtic manufactures and foreign trade, it is not too much to
aſſert, that it muſt have added to its houſes and
people one-fourth, ſince 1750 ‡.

But,

---

* The country commiſſioners, often diſcharge on appeal,
houſes, as not properly chargeable. This may occaſion an
apparent decreaſe.

† In the *villages around London*, there were baptiſed, during a period of twenty years, beginning with the Revolution - - - - 20,782
During 20 years, beginning with 1758—60, or 61 39,383

‡ In ſixteen pariſhes in Lancaſhire, excluſive of Mancheſter
and Liverpool, there were baptiſed in twenty years,
about the Revolution - - 18,389
Ditto, from 1758 - - - - 47,919

Theſe proofs of a rapid increaſe of natural population are
from Mr. Howlet's Examination. It is an acknowledged fact,
that Liverpool has doubled its inhabitants every five-and-
twenty years, ſince the year 1700.

Of

But, it is said to be idle and impertinent to argue from the state of population in Yorkshire, or in Lancashire, since Doctor Price is ready to admit, *that these have added many to their numbers* *. Yet, owing to what *moral cause* is it, that York and Lancashire, Chester and Derby, have acquired so many people? Is it owing to their manufactories, and traffic, and navigation, which augmented employments? Now, the same causes have produced the same effects, in the other counties of this for-

Of houses it contained, in 1753 — 3,700
in 1773 — 5,929
in 1783 — 6,819
Yet were its houses returned to the tax-office,
in 1777 at 3,974
and in 1784 at 4,489
Manchester with Salford have equally increased.
Of houses there were in both, in 1773 — 4,268
in 1783 — 6,178;
Of which there were returned to the tax-office,
in 1777 — 2,519
in 1784 — 3,665

And it might be easily shewn, that the smaller towns and villages of Lancashire have grown nearly in the same proportion; and this most prosperous county has, during the last ninety years, increased in the numbers of people with the boasted rapidity of the American states. Bolton (in New-England) was settled in 1633; yet, it did not contain twenty thousand inhabitants in 1775. Philadelphia was planted in 1682; yet, in its happiest days, it did not comprehend forty thousand souls. The other towns of the American states, being much inferior to these, can still less be compared to the manufacturing villages of England, or to Paisley, in Scotland.

* Uncertainty of Population, p. 14—19.

O tunate

tunate ifland, in proportion as thefe caufes have prevailed in each.

It is pretended, however, that the aftonifhing augmentation of our cities did not arife from births amidft profperity and happinefs, fince many people were brought from other diftricts by the allurements of gain. The additional labourers could not affuredly have come, in confiderable numbers, from thofe counties, which have fuftained no diminution of people themfelves: and in no European country is there lefs migration from one parifh to another, than in England. The principle of the poor laws checks population, by preventing the laborious poor from looking for better employment beyond the limits of their native parifhes. Every one knows with what tyrannic rigour *the law of fettlements* is enforced, by fending to their proper parifhes the adventurous perfons, who had found no employment at home. It is not therefore the migration of the adult from the country to the town, that continually fwells the amount of the bufy multitudes, which are feen to fwarm where the fpirit of diligence animates the people: and it is the employment and habits of induftry, which are given to children in manufacturing towns, that add to the aggregate of dwellers in them, more than the arrival of ftrangers.

Having, in the foregoing manner, traced a gradual progrefs from *The Conqueft* to *The Revolution*; having thus eftablifhed, by the beft proofs which fuch an inquiry, without enumerations, admits,

that

that the former current of population not only continued to run, but acquired a rapidity and a fulnefs as it flowed; we fhall not find it difficult,
fince the chief objections are removed, to afcertain
the probable amount of the prefent inhabitants.
He who infifts, that there were in England and
Wales 1,300,000 inhabited houfes in 1688, muft
equally allow, fince it has been proved, that of
thefe there were 711,000, which were inhabited by
perfons, who either received alms, or gave none;
and it has been equally fhewn, that the neceffary
labour of the prefent day could not, by any poffible exertions, be performed by the lower orders,
who certainly exifted in 1688. Hence, it is reafonable to conclude, that, fince the 590,000 *chargeable* houfes, in 1690, were accompanied with
710,000 *dwellings of the poor*, the 721,000 *chargeable* houfes of 1781, muft confequently be accompanied with 865,000 *dwellings of the poor*. For,
fuch is the inference of juft proportion. The diftinct dwellings in England and Wales, when both
claffes are added together, muft be 1,586,000;
which, if multiplied by $5\frac{1}{7}$, for the number of perfons in each, would difcover the whole numbers to
be 8,447,200 : But, there ought ftill to be an adequate allowance for empty houfes, and for other
circumftances of diminution; which, after every
deduction, would fhew the prefent population of
England and Wales to be rather more than eight
million. And fuch an augmentation, as this
would evince, fince the Revolution, is altogether

confiftent

confiftent with reafon, with facts, and with experience.

Mr. Wallace, the learned antagonift of Mr.
Hume, very juftly remarks *, " that it is not owing
" to the want of prolific virtue, but, to the dif-
" treffed circumftances of mankind, every genera-
" tion do not more than double themfelves; which
" would be the cafe, if every man were married
" at the age of puberty, and could provide for a
" family." He plainly evinces, that there might
have eafily proceeded from the *created pair*
6,291,456 perfons in feven hundred years. From
the foregoing difcuffions we have feen an augmentation of four million and a half of people, during
fix centuries and a quarter, of tyranny, of war, and
of peftilence. But, when we confider the more
frequent employments and agreeable comforts of
the people, their fuperior freedom and greater
healthfulnefs, we may affuredly conclude, that there
has been an augmentation of a million and a half
fince *The Revolution.*

Of this gradual increafe of people, Ireland furnifhes a remarkable example, though this kingdom
has not always enjoyed, during the effluxion of the
laft century, a fituation equally fortunate †. Ireland

* Differt. on the Numbers of Mankind, p. 8.
† Though the hearth-books of England have funk into
oblivion, the hearth-books of Ireland remain. From the produce of the hearth-tax may be traced its gradual rife, as in
the fubjoined detail, which evinces the progrefs of population.

(197)

land has fuffered, during this period, the miferies
of civil war, which ended in the forfeiture and ex-
pulfion of thoufands. In this period alfo multitudes conftantly emigrated, either to exercife their
induftry, or to draw the fword in foreign climes.
Yet, are there abundant reafons to believe, that this
prolific ifland has much more than doubled its inhabitants in the laft hundred years.

Sir William Petty, who poffeffed very minute
details with regard to the condition of Ireland,
from the Reftoration to the Revolution, ftates the
number of houfes, in 1672*, at   - - 200,020
The number returned by the tax-gather-
    ers, in 1781 †, was   -   -   -   -   477,602

At the firft epoch, the Irifh nation had fcarcely re-
covered from a long and deftructive civil war. It
is fufficiently known, that in the accounts of 1781,
there are many houfes omitted, which often happens, when intereft may be promoted by conceal-

tion. It yielded, according to a five years average, ending
with   —   —   —   1687   —— £. 32,416
Three years average, with   1732   ——   42,456
D°   —   —   with   1762   ——   55,189
Seven years   —   d°   —   1777   ——   59,869
Five years   —   d°   —   1781   ——   60,648
                 In 1781   ——   63,820

See Bibl. Harl. Brit. Muf. N° 4706—Mr. A. Young's Tour in
Ireland, the Appendix—and Mr. Howlet's Effay on the Popu-
lation of Ireland, juft publifhed, p. 19.
* Pol. Anatomy, p. 7-11-17-116.
† Mr. Howlet's Effay on the Population of Ireland, p. 13.

O 3   ment.

ment. Sir William Petty ſtates the whole population of Ireland, in 1672, at - 1,100,000 ſouls.
Were we to multiply 478,000
  houſes of the preſent day, at
  5½ in each, this would carry
the number up to   -   - 2,550,000

And the moſt intelligent perſons in that kingdom
ſuppoſe Ireland to contain about two millions and
a half of ſouls *. Were we to admit this as merely an approximation to truth, this would evince a
ſtill more conſiderable increaſe of people, than, as
we have ſo many reaſons for believing, took place
during the laſt hundred years in England, which
enjoyed more productive advantages. This example ought to be more convincing than many arguments.

The ſame principles, which in every age influenced the population of England, produced ſimilar
effects on the populouſneſs of Scotland. When
England was poor and depopulated, we may eaſily
conjecture, that Scotland could not have been very
opulent or populous. And, as England gradually
acquired inhabitants, we may preſume Scotland
followed her track, though at a great diſtance be-
hind. An intelligent obſerver might form a ſatiſ-
factory judgment of the previous condition of the
two kingdoms, from the accurate ſtatements
whereon their union was formed.

* Mr. A. Young's Tour in Ireland, the Appendix.

The

The public revenue of England was £. 5,691,803
of Scotland - - 160,000

Of the trade of both we may determine
from the cuftom-houfe duties, which
in England were - - - £. 1,341,559
in Scotland - - - - 34,000

The grofs income of the pofts was,
in England - - - £. 101,101
in Scotland - - - 1,194

Of the circulation of both we may form
an opinion from the re-coinage of
both. There were re-coined in England, during King William's reign £. 8,400,000
In Scotland, foon after the Union - 411,118

We may decide with regard to the confumption of both from the excife-
duties; which in England amounted
to - - - £. 947,602
in Scotland to - - 33,500

From thefe details * it is reafonable to infer, that
Scotland poffeffed, in thofe days, no flourifhing hufbandry, few manufactories, little commerce, and
lefs circulation, though there had certainly been a
confiderable advance, in all thefe, during the two

* See the elaborate and very curious Hiftory of the Union
by De Foe, juft re-publifhed by Stockdale.

preceding

preceding centuries. "Numbers of people, the
"greateſt riches of other nations," ſaid Mr. Law *,
in 1705, "are a burden to us; the land is not
"improved; the produ&t is not manufactured;
"the fiſhing, and other advantages of foreign trade
"are neglected." Such was the denlorable ſtate
of Scotland at the epoch of its happy union with
England.

The Scots were for years too much engaged in
religious and political controverſy, to derive from
that fortunate event, all the advantages which, at
length, have undoubtedly flowed from it. Their
misfortunes, ariſing chiefly from theſe evils, have,
however, conferred on them the moſt invigorating
benefits. The laws that a wiſe policy enacted,
created greater perſonal independence, and eſtabliſhed better ſafeguards for property, which have
produced the uſual effects of a more animating induſtry. Of the intermediate improvements of their
tillage we may form ſome judgment from the riſe of
rents, and the advance of the purchaſe money for
land, which muſt have neceſſarily proceeded from a
better huſbandry, or a greater opulence. The manufactures, which the Scotch doubtleſs poſſeſſed, in
1707, though to no conſiderable extent, have not
only been greatly enlarged †, but to the old, new
ones

* Conſiderations on Money and Trade.
† The quantity of linen made for ſale in Scotland, during
1728, was only 2,000,000 yards; but, in 1775, 12,000,000.
The linen is the chief manufacture of Scotland; and, were

2   we

ones have mean while been added. The value of the whole exports by fea, amounted, at the epoch of the Union, if we may believe Mr. Law, to about £. 300,000 : The whole of thefe exports were carried up, before the colonywar began, to £.1,800,000, if we may credit the cuftom-houfe books. The tonnage of fhipping, which annually entered the ports of Scotland, at the firft æra, was only 10,000*; but, at the laft, 93,000 tons. The foregoing ftatements, general as they are, will evince to every intelligent mind, how much the

we to regard this as a proper reprefentative of the whole, we might from this infer a very confiderable augmentation in every other manufacture.

* In the Harl. MSS. No. 6269, Brit. Muf. there is a lift of the fhips belonging to Scotland, (as they were entered in the Regifter General kept at London) and Trading in the ports of that kingdom, from Chriftmas 1707, to Chriftmas 1712, diftinguifhing thofe belonging to Scotland, prior to the Union, as follows :

	Veffels.	Tons:
Total - - - -	1,123 —	50,232
Prior to the Union -	- 215 —	14,485
Increafe -	908 —	35,747

There belonged to Scotland, in 1784, of veffels, which entered only once - - 1,649 — 92,349;

Of which were employed

	Veffels.	Tons.
in foreign trade -	643 —	50,386
Coaft trade - -	709 —	31,542
Fifhing fhallops, &c.	297 —	10,421
	1,649 —	92,349.

Thefe comparative ftatements evince undoubtedly a very confiderable increafe of fhipping in the intermediate period.

commerce

commerce and navigation of Scotland have increafed, fince the hearts and hands of the two
kingdoms were fortunately joined together.

Of the traffic of Scotland, it ought to be however
remarked, that it is more eafily driven from its
courfe than the Englifh, either by internal misfortunes, or by foreign warfare; becaufe it is lefs
firmly eftablifhed; it is fupported by fmaller capitals; and its range is lefs extenfive. The bankruptcies of 1772 deduƈted nearly £. 300,000 from
the annual exports of Scotland. The commercial
events of our two laft wars would alone juftify
this remark. Let us compare, then, the exports
of Scotland, when they were the loweft, during the
war of 1755, with the loweft exports of the colony-war, and the higheft exports of the firft, with
the higheft of the fecond; becaufe we fhall thereby fee the depreffions and elevations of both:

The Value of Exports,

in 1755 – £.535,577 — in 1782 – £.653,709
in 1756 –   628,049 — in 1778 –   702,820
in 1757 –   828,577 — in 1781 –   763,809

in 1760 – 1,086,205 — in 1776 – 1,025,973
in 1761 – 1,165,722 — in 1777 –   837,643
in 1762 –   998,165 — in 1780 – 1,002,039

When we recolleƈt, that Great Britain was engaged, during the laft war with her colonies, which
occupied fo much of the foreign trade of Scotland, with France, with Spain, and with Holland,

2   we

we ought not to be furprifed, that fo much fhould be loft, as that fo much fhould remain, after feven years hoftilities. It was deranged, but it was not ruined, as had been predicted, in 1774. And, when the various preffures of this moft diftrefsful war were removed, though with a tardy hand, it began to rife, yet not with the elafticity of 1763, becaufe the colony commerce, which furnifhed fo many of the exports of Scotland, had been turned into other channels. But, the following detail will enable us to form a more accurate judgment, with regard to this interefting fubject :

The Value of Exports from Scotland,
in 1762 - £.998,165 — in 1782 - £.653,709
in 1763 - 1,091,436 — in 1783 - 829,824
in 1764 - 1,243,927 — in 1784 - 929,900

It ought however to be remembered, that in the firft period, complete peace was eftablifhed in 1763; but, in the laft, it was not fully reftored till the middle of 1784. Yet, the fhipping of Scotland will be found, as we have already perceived them to be in England, our moft infallible guides; becaufe, the entries of fhips are more accurately taken than the value of cargoes, and trade can fcarcely be faid to decline while our veffels increafe. Let us attend, then, to the following detail of fhips, which entered in the ports of Scotland, during the following years, both before and after war :

	Foreign Trade.	Coaſt Trade.	Fiſhing, &c.
in 1769 -	48,271 tons.	21,615 tons.	10,275 tons.
in 1774 -	52,225 —	26,214 —	14,903
in 1784 -	50,386 —	31,542 —	*10,421

It is apparent then, that though the foreign trade of Scotland was ſomewhat inferior, in 1784, to that of 1774, it was equally ſuperior to that of 1769 : That the coaſt trade was much greater, in 1784, than ever it had been in any prior year : And, that the fiſhing buſineſs of 1784 was more extenſive than it had been in 1769, but much more confined than in 1774, if we may implicitly credit the cuſtom-houſe books.

However the foreign trade of Scotland may have been depreſſed by the colony-war, there is reaſon to believe, that ſhe has thereby added to her domeſtic manufactures. The commercial capitals, which could no longer be employed abroad, were at length more uſefully laid out at home.

* The cuſtom-houſe account, from which the above detail is taken, ſtates the ſhips *to belong to Scotland,* accounting each *veſſel only one voyage in every year.* This comparative eſtimate of the ſhipping, which were employed in the foreign or overſea trade of Scotland, may be carried back to the peace of 1763. Thus there were employed,

in 1759 — 29,902 tons. — in 1761 — 31,411 tons.
in 1763 — 33,352 — in 1764 — 41,076

Whence we may undoubtedly conclude, that Scotland poſſeſſes a much greater navigation at preſent, than at the peace of 1763, or at any prior epoch.

Inſtead

Inſtead of promoting the labour of other countries,
theſe capitals furniſhed employment to many
hands, within the kingdom. And Scotland has
by this means extended her valuable manufacture
of gauzes ; ſhe has augmented the number of her
print-fields ; ſhe has acquired every branch of the
cotton buſineſs ; and ſhe has greatly increaſed her
linens *. Thus it is, that an active people may
be even enriched, by throwing obſtructions in the
way of their foreign commerce. And, if productive labour conſtitutes genuine wealth, the Scots
may be regarded at preſent as a nation more induſtrious and opulent than they were before the
colony-war began.

Theſe obſervations apply equally to England.
Every occurrence, which at any time turned additional capitals into domeſtic employments, necef-
ſarily contributed to improve the agriculture, to
augment the manufactures, and to increaſe the
wealth of the country, by yielding a greater
quantity of productive labour. A review of the
foregoing documents would illuſtrate this ſubject.
As a ſupplemental proof, I have annexed *a chrono-*

* Of Linens there were made for ſale ;

in 1772 - 13,089,006 yards. - in 1782 - 15,348,744 yards.
  1773 - 10,748,110   —   1783 - 17,074,777
  1774 - 11,422,115   —   1784 - 19,138,593

The greater number of ſhipping, which are at preſent employed, than before the war, in the coaſt-trade of Scotland,
ſeems alſo to evince an augmentation of domeſtic commerce.

logical

logical *account of commerce*, in this island, from the
Reftoration to the year 1785, with defign to exhibit
a more connected view of the weaknefs of its commencement, the ftruggles of its progreffion, and
the greatnefs of its maturity, than has yet been
done:

A CHRO-

A CHR[...] om the Reſtoration to the Year 1785.

Epochs.	Total.	Nett Cuſtoms paid into the Exchequer.	Money coined.
ιε Reſtoration,	1 —— 1 ——	£. 390,000	By Charles II. - - - £. 7,584,105
ιε Revolution,	1 ——	551,141	By James II. - - - 2,737,637
xce of Ryſwick,	1 £. 43,320	694,892	£. 10,261,742
4 Years of William III.	1 1,386,832	1,474,861	By William III. - - £. 10,511,963
ιη of Anne,	2 2,116,451 / 3 3,014,175	1,257,332 / 1,315,423	By Anne, - - - £. 2,691,626
4 of George I.	1 1,904,151	1,588,162	By George I. - - £. 8,725,921
4 of George II.	1 3,514,768	1,621,731	
xtful Years,	1 4,642,502	1,492,009	
r of —	1 2,455,313	1,399,865	
xtful Years,	1 6,521,964	1,565,942	
r of —	1 4,046,465	1,763,314	By George II. { Gold, £. 11,662,216 / Silver, - - 304,360
4 of George III.	1 5,981,682	1,969,934	£. 11,966,576
	7,239,133	1,866,152	
	5,553,098	1,858,417	
	4,682,691	2,249,604	
	6,505,671	2,169,473	
	3,919,230	2,271,231	
	2,731,904	2,448,280	
	1,992,848	2,355,850	
	3,504,823	2,445,016	
	1,867,199	2,639,086	
	2,564,272	2,546,144	
	4,810,156	2,642,129	
	3,211,453	2,525,596	
	3,852,783	2,435,017	
	3,058,544	2,567,770	
	2,275,003	2,481,031	By George III. before the 31ſt of Dec. 1780. { Gold, £. 30,457,805 / Silver, - 7,126
	3,241,716	2,480,403	
	1,508,385	2,229,106	£. 30,464,931
	1,379,653	2,162,681	
	2,154,634	2,502,274	From 31 Dec. 1780, to 1 Jan. 1785. { in Gold, £. 2,624,079 / in Silver, - - 264
	1,787,809	2,723,920	
		2,791,428	£. 2,624,343
	2,823,143	2,861,563	
	1,737,027	2,848,320	Total to 1 January, 1785 £. 33,089,274
	52,209	3,326,639	

A CHRONOLOGICAL ACCOUNT of COMMERCE in this

Epochs.		Ships cleared outwards.			Value of Cargoes exported.			B
		Tons English.	D° foreign.	Total.	English.	Scotch.	Total.	English.
Restoration,	1663 / 1669	95,266 —	47,634 —	142,900 —	£.2,043,043 —	—	£.2,043,043 —	Unfavourable.
Revolution,	1688 —	190,533 —	95,267 —	285,800 —	4,086,087 —	—	4,086,087 —	Doubtful.
of Ryswick,	1697 —	144,264 —	100,524 —	244,788 —	3,525,907 —	—	3,525,907 —	£.43,320
Years of William III.	1700 / 01 / 02	273,693 —	43,635 —	317,328 —	6,045,432 —	—	6,045,432 —	1,386,832
of Anne,	1709 / 1712	243,693 — / 326,620 —	45,625 — / 29,115 —	289,318 — / 355,735 —	5,913,357 / 6,868,840 —	—	5,913,357 / 6,868,840 —	2,116,451 / 3,014,175
of George I.	1713 / 14 / 15	421,431 —	26,573 —	448,004 —	7,696,573 —	—	7,696,573 —	1,904,151
of George II.	1726 / 27 / 28	432,832 —	23,651 —	456,483 —	7,891,739 —	—	7,891,739 —	3,514,768
Years,	1736 / 37 / 38	476,941 —	26,627 —	503,568 —	9,993,232 —	—	9,993,232 —	4,642,502
—	1739 / 40 / 41	384,191 —	87,260 —	471,451 —	8,870,499 —	—	8,870,499 —	2,455,313
Years,	1749 / 50 / 51	609,798 —	51,386 —	661,184 —	12,599,112 —	—	12,599,112 —	6,521,964
—	1755 / 56 / 57	451,254 —	73,456 —	524,710 —	11,708,515 —	663,401 —	12,371,916 —	4,046,465
of George III.	1760 —	471,241 —	102,737 —	573,978 —	14,694,970 —	1,086,205 —	15,781,175 —	5,746,270
	61 —	508,220 —	117,835 —	626,055 —	14,873,191 —	1,165,722 —	16,038,913 —	6,822,051
	62 —	480,444 —	120,126 —	600,570 —	13,545,171 —	998,165 —	14,543,336 —	5,263,858
	63 —	561,724 —	87,293 —	649,017 —	14,487,507 —	1,091,436 —	15,578,943 —	4,495,146
	64 —	583,934 —	74,800 —	658,734 —	16,512,404 —	1,243,927 —	17,756,331 —	6,148,096
	65 —	651,402 —	67,855 —	719,257 —	14,550,507 —	1,180,867 —	15,731,374 —	3,660,764
	66 —	684,281 —	61,753 —	746,034 —	14,024,964 —	1,163,704 —	15,188,668 —	2,549,189
	67 —	645,835 —	63,206 —	709,041 —	13,844,511 —	1,245,490 —	15,090,001 —	1,770,555
	68 —	668,786 —	72,734 —	741,520 —	15,117,983 —	1,502,150 —	16,620,133 —	3,239,322
	69 —	709,855 —	63,020 —	772,875 —	13,438,236 —	1,563,053 —	15,001,289 —	1,529,676
	1770 —	703,495 —	57,476 —	760,971 —	14,266,654 —	1,729,915 —	15,996,569 —	2,049,716
	71 —	773,390 —	63,532 —	836,922 —	17,161,147 —	1,857,334 —	19,018,481 —	4,339,151
	72 —	818,108 —	72,603 —	890,711 —	16,159,413 —	1,560,756 —	17,720,169 —	2,860,961
	73 —	771,483 —	54,820 —	826,303 —	14,763,253 —	1,612,175 —	16,375,428 —	3,356,412
	74 —	798,240 —	65,273 —	863,513 —	15,916,344 —	1,372,143 —	17,288,487 —	2,888,678
	75 —	783,226 —	64,860 —	848,086 —	15,202,366 —	1,123,998 —	16,326,364 —	2,275,003
	76 —	778,878 —	72,188 —	851,066 —	13,729,726 —	1,025,973 —	14,755,699 —	2,962,424
	77 —	736,234 —	83,468 —	819,702 —	12,653,363 —	837,643 —	13,491,006 —	1,472,996
	78 —	657,238 —	98,113 —	755,351 —	11,551,070 —	702,820 —	12,253,890 —	1,379,653
	79 —	590,911 —	139,124 —	730,035 —	12,693,430 —	837,273 —	13,530,703 —	2,092,133
	1780 —	619,462 —	134,515 —	753,977 —	11,621,333 —	1,002,039 —	12,624,372 —	1,688,494
	81 —	547,953 —	163,410 —	711,363 —	10,569,187 —	763,109 —	11,332,296 —	
	82 —	552,851 —	208,511 —	761,362 —	12,355,750 —	651,709 —	13,009,459 —	2,853,143
	83 —	795,669 —	157,969 —	953,638 —	13,851,671 —	829,824 —	14,681,495 —	1,737,027
	84 —	846,355 —	113,064 —	959,419 —	14,171,375 —	929,900 —	15,101,275 —	52,209

...ported. Total.	Balance of Trade.			Nett Customs paid into the Exchequer.	Money coined.
	English.	Scotch.	Total.		
3,043,043	Unfavourable.			£. 390,000	By Charles II. - - £. 7,584,105
4,086,087	Doubtful.			551,141	By James II. - - 2,737,637
3,525,907	£. 43,320		£. 43,320	694,892	£. 10,261,742
6,045,432	1,386,832		1,386,832	1,474,861	By William III. - - £. 10,511,963
5,415,157	2,116,451		2,116,451	1,257,332	
6,865,840	3,014,175		3,014,175	1,315,423	By Anne, - - - £. 2,691,626
7,696,573	1,904,151		1,904,151	1,588,162	By George I. - - £. 8,725,981
7,891,739	3,514,768		3,514,768	1,621,731	
9,993,232	4,642,502		4,642,502	1,492,009	
8,870,499	2,455,313		2,455,313	1,399,865	
12,599,112	6,521,964		6,521,964	1,565,942	
12,371,916	4,046,465		4,046,465	1,763,314	By George II. { Gold, £. 11,662,216 / Silver, - - 304,360
15,781,175	5,746,270	235,412	5,981,682	1,969,934	£. 11,966,576
16,038,913	6,822,051	417,082	7,239,133	1,866,152	
14,543,336	5,263,858	289,240	5,553,098	1,858,417	
15,578,943	4,495,146	187,545	4,682,691	2,249,604	
17,756,331	6,148,096	357,575	6,505,671	2,169,473	
15,731,374	3,660,764	258,466	3,919,230	2,271,231	
15,188,668	2,549,189	182,715	2,731,904	2,448,280	
15,090,001	1,770,555	222,293	1,992,848	2,355,850	
16,620,133	3,239,322	265,501	3,504,823	2,445,016	
15,001,289	1,529,676	337,523	1,867,199	2,639,086	
15,996,569	2,049,716	514,556	2,564,272	2,566,144	
19,018,481	4,339,151	471,005	4,810,156	2,642,129	
17,720,169	2,860,961	350,492	3,211,453	2,525,596	
16,375,428	3,356,412	496,376	3,852,783	2,439,017	
17,288,487	2,888,678	169,866	3,058,544	2,567,770	
16,326,164	2,275,003		2,275,003	2,481,031	By George III. before the 31st of Dec. 1780. { Gold, £. 30,457,802 / Silver, - 7,128
14,755,699	1,962,424	279,292	3,241,716	2,480,403	£. 30,464,931
13,491,006	1,472,996	35,389	1,508,385	2,229,106	
12,253,890	1,379,653		1,379,653	2,162,681	
13,530,703	2,092,133	62,501	2,154,634	2,502,274	From 31 Dec. 1780, to 1 Jan. 1785. { in Gold, £. 2,624,079 / in Silver, - - 264
12,624,372	1,688,494	99,315	1,787,809	2,723,920	£. 2,624,343
11,332,296				2,791,428	
13,009,459	2,823,143		2,823,143	2,861,563	
14,681,495	1,737,027		1,737,027	2,848,320	Total to 1 January, 1785 £. 33,089,274
15,101,275	52,209		52,209	3,326,639	

Of the annexed table, the eye inftantly perceives
the difpofition of the parts and the arrangement of
the whole. In the firft column may be feen the various epochs, beginning with the Reftoration, whence
certainty may be faid to commence, and ending
with the year 1784, becaufe here our documents
fail, as the public accounts are yet brought no
lower down. The fecond column gives the tonnage of the fhipping that fucceffively failed from
England, diftinguifhing the Englifh from the foreign, in order to find, in the amount of each,
the falutary effects of the act of navigation. The
third column contains the value of the merchandize fent out, that the extent of the cargoes may
be compared with the quantity of tonnage which
carried them : and, though the Scotch tonnage
could not be adjoined, the value of the Scotch exports is added, becaufe every one finds a gratification in extending his views. The fourth column
exhibits the refult of our exports and imports
compared, which forms what has been denomi-
nated the balance of trade. The fifth column
ftates the nett cuftoms, which our foreign commerce has yielded at different periods, becaufe,
while the detail gratifies curiofity, it furnifhes no
inconfiderable proof of the profperity or decline of
our traffic. And the laft column contains, what
may be regarded as the refult of the whole, the
fums which have been coined in England, during
every reign fubfequent to the Reftoration ; becaufe *the mint*, as Sir Robert Cotton expreffes it, *is
the pulfe of the commonwealth.*

That

That the progrefs of our traffic and navigation, from the commencement of the feventeenth century to the æra of the Reftoration, had been remarkably rapid, all mercantile writers feem to admit. The navigation act contributed greatly to carry this advance up to the Revolution. Sir William Petty ftated, in 1670, " that the fhipping of England had trebled in forty years." Doctor Davenant afterwards afferted *, " that experienced merchants did agree, that we had, in 1688, near double the tonnage of trading fhipping to what we had in 1666. And Anderfon † inferred, from the concurring teftimony of authors on this interefting fubject, " that the Englifh nation was in the zenith of commercial profperity at the Revolution." We have already examined how much the commercial gain of our traders was taken away by the war which immediately followed that moft important event in our annals. But the eye muft be again thrown over the chronological table, if the reader wifhes for a more comprehenfive view of the continual progrefs of navigation, from the ftation of eminence to which Anderfon had traced it; its temporary interruptions; and its final exaltation, fince the independence of the American ftates. If we compare the greatnefs of 1688, with the amount of 1774 and 1784, we fhall difcover that the navigation of the latter epochs had reached a point of the mercantile heavens fo much more exalted than the former, as to

* Vol. ii. p. 29.   † Commerce, vol. ii. p. 187.

reverfe

reverfe its pofition; as to convert what was once *the zenith* into *the nadir* now.

	Tons Englifh.	D° foreign.	Total.
Contraſt 1688 —	190,533 —	95,267 —	285,800
with 1774 —	798,240 —	65,273 —	863,513
with 1784 —	846,355 —	113,064 —	959,419

The famous Mr. Gregory King calculated [*], "*that we gained annually on the freight of Englifh fhipping,* in 1688, — — — £. 810,000." If the " *national profit on the naval trade of England, in* 1688," amounted to £. 810,000, what ought to have been *the national profit on our naval trade in* 1774? If 190,000 tons gained £. 810,000, 790,000 tons muſt have gained - £. 3,367,889. 940,000 tons, including the Scots fhips, muſt alfo have gained, in 1784 — — — —£. 4,060,000.

This is doubtlefs a vaſt fum to be annually gained from our outward freights; but, great as it appears, when the fame fum is added for our inward freights, in a mere mercantile light, the immenfe navigation, from whence it arifes, muſt be confidered as ſtill more advantageous to the ſtate, as a never-failing fource, from which feamen

---

* Dav. Works, vol. vi. p. 146.

and

and tranfports may be conftantly drawn fpr-the ufes of war. If from the tonnage, which may be moft fafely followed in difcovering the benefits of our navigation and commerce, during every age, we look into the *column of cargoes*, in the chronological table, we fhall find an excellent auxiliary, in the ledger of the infpector-general, for conducting our inquiries and informing our judgments.

To inveftigate the value of our exports and of our imports, during the difturbed times of our Edwards and Henries, or even in the placid days of Elizabeth, would be a refearch of curiofity rather than of ufe. On a fubject of. fuch difficult difcuffion, as no fufficient data had yet been eftablifhed, the moft judicious calculators could only fpeak in terms indefinite, and therefore unfatisfactory: yet, Sir William Petty, Sir Jofiah Child, Dr. Davenant, and Mr. Locke, all agreed in afferting, that our commerce flourifhed extremely from 1666 to 1688, when it had increafed beyond all former example; and when its general growth, in the opinion of the moft experienced merchants, was double in its magnitude at the Revolution, to its ufual fize at the Reftoration. In the chronological table, the value of exported commodities was adjufted for both thefe periods, by a ftandard, which feems to be thus admitted as equal, by the wifeft men in England.

During that day of commercial darknefs, the experienced Sir Phillip Meadows, whofe prefence for fo many years did honour to the Board of

Trade,

Trade, fat down to form "*a general eſtimate of the trade of England,*" from the amount of the duties paid at the cuſtom-houſe on our importations and on our exports. Directed by his native ſagacity, he produced a ſtatement of our commerce on an average of the three years of war 1694—5—6; which appears now, from a comparifon with the entries in the ledger of the infpector-general, to have been wonderfully exact.

Value of exports *, according to Sir Philip's
  calculation,   —   —   £. 3,124,000
D°, according to the ledger, from
  Michaelmas 1696 to D° 1697,   3,525,907

Value of imports, according to
  him,   —   —   —   £. 3,050,000
D°, according to the ledger, —   3,482,587
Favourable balance of trade, ac-
  cording to him,   —   — £.   74,000
D°, according to the ledger, —   43,341

In the foregoing detail, from which we afcertain by comparifon nearly the truth, we behold

---

* But Sir P. Meadows excluded from his calculation the value of butter, cheefe, candles, beef, pork, and other proviſions exported to the Plantations, and the value of their products imported into England, which were afterwards confumed ; " being in the nature of our coaſt-trade among our own people." Had he included thefe, his ſtatement had been ſtill nearer in its amount to the ledger of the infpector-general.

         the

the inconfiderable extent of the national commerce at the peace of Ryfwick. *If,* faid that able ftatef-man, *the prefent condition of England be not fatis-factory to the public, from the general account of it here mentioned,* various ways may be followed to im-prove it: And his fuggeftions having been gradu-ally adopted in after times, produced at length the wifhed-for effects of an active induftry at home, and a profperous navigation abroad. From that epoch, we have in the books of the infpector-general all the certainty, with regard to the annual amount of our exports and our imports, which the nature of fuch compli-cated tranfactions eafily admit. But, fhould the nation wifh for more fatisfactory evidence, on a fubject fo interefting, becaufe it involves in it the welfare of the ftate, the fame motion, which was made in the Houfe of Commons by Mr. Lownds *, during the reign of Queen Anne, to oblige the traders to make true entries of their cargoes, may be again propofed, and, if it can be freed from objection, carried into effect by par-liamentary regulations.

Mean time, the tonnage of fhipping, which tranfported the fuperfluous products of England, has been adjoined, in the foregoing table, to the value of cargoes, in order to fupply any defect of

---

* "In order to prevent this mifchief [of exaggerated entries] fays Davenant, a claufe was offered, and very much infifted on by Mr. Lownds, but obftructed by the merchants, for ends not very juftifiable, and the claufe was not received."—Dav. vol. v. Whitworth's edit. p. 443.

proof,

proof, and to corroborate the certainty of each
by a fair comparifon of both. When Sir Philip
Meadows confidered, with fo much attention,
our commercial affairs, he gave it as his opinion,
" that the advantage of trade cannot be computed
by any general meafure better than by that of
the navigation." It requires not, indeed, the
grafp of Sir Philip's mind to perceive, that the
tonnage is naturally the evidence the moft to be
relied on, where there is any doubt : in this mode
of proof there is no fiction : the entries are made
at the Cuftom-houfe, on the oath of the mafters ;
yet the tonnage is fuppofed to contain about one-
third lefs than the truth : but, the general average being once known and admitted, we may
argue from the apparent amount, with no more
dread of deception, than we fhould expect from
the notices of the moft authentic record. In
comparing the value of the cargoes with the extent of the tonnage, as both are ftated in the
foregoing table, we ought to infer that the firft
muft always be fuperior in its rifings and depreffions to the laft. It was with a view to this
comparifon and correfpondence, that the bullion,
whofe annual exportation for fo many years
frightened the graveft politicians, was deducted
from the value of the tranfported merchandize ;
fince it occupied little room in the tonnage, yet
fwelled confiderably the calculation of the general
cargo : But, the exported bullion was retained in
forming the balances of trade, becaufe, though it
cannot properly be confidered as a manufacture, it

P 3   ought

ought nevertheless to be deemed a very valuable part of our actual wealth, which we send abroad in expectation of a profitable return.

Thus, we see in the foregoing documents *the best evidence*, with regard to our navigation and our trade, *that the nature of the enquiry admits.* He who wishes to satisfy his doubts, or to gain information, by throwing his eye over the state of our exports from 1696 to 1774, as it has been published by Sir Charles Whitworth; or the value of cargoes which have been exported during the present reign, as they have been arranged in the foregoing table; must perceive, that when one year furnishes a great exportation, the next supplies the foreign markets with less; the third usually sends a cargo superior to the first; and the fourth gives often a smaller quantity than the last, whose amount however is seldom below the level of the first. This striking variation arises chiefly from the irregularities of universal demand, since foreign fairs are sometimes empty and sometimes full; and partly from the speculations, perhaps the caprice, of traders. And it has been shewn from the most satisfactory proofs, that the year of profound peace, which immediately succeeds the conclusion of a lengthened war, always furnishes a great exportation, because every merchant makes haste to be rich: Thus, 1698, 1714, 1749, 1764, and 1784, form epochs of great relative traffic. But it is from the averages of distant years, at given periods, that we can only form a decided opinion with regard to the real prosperity or de-

cay

cay either of commerce, or of navigation : Thus,
from the Reſtoration to the Revolution, the foreign trade of England had doubled in its amount:
from the peace of Ryſwick to the demiſe of King
William, it had nearly riſen in the ſame proportion. During the firſt thirty years of the current
century, it had again doubled : and from the year
1750 to 1774, notwithſtanding the interruptions
of an eight-years intervenient war, it appears to
have gained more than one-fourth, whether we determine from the table of tonnage *, or the value of exports.

Though the late war ſeems to have been le-
velled rather againſt the induſtry of the manufac-
turer and the projects of the merchant, than
againſt the force of our fleets or the power of our
armies ; though repeated blows of unuſual ſeverity
have been given to our navigation and our trade ;
yet, our domeſtic diligence purſues with unabated
ardour its uſual occupations ; the number of our
ſhipping at preſent is great beyond example ; and
our trade, which was ſaid to be almoſt undone,
ſtill riſes ſuperior to its various oppreſſions. Let
theſe conſiderations comfort every lover of his
country, ſince it is as difficult to animate the de-
ſpondent, as it is to convince the incredulous.

If from theſe exhilarating topics, we turn to the
column in the chronological table, which is occupied by the balance of trade, we ſhall find rather
a more melancholy topic. No diſquiſition has

* See the annexed Table.

P 4   engaged

engaged the pens of a more numerous claſs of
writers than that fruitful ſubjeƈt; who all complained of the difficulty of their labours, as they
were each direƈted by feeble lights; and who warn-
ed their readers of the uncertainty of their concluſions, becauſe their calculations had been formed
on very diſputable data.

In reviewing their performances, how amuſing is
it to obſerve, that though the ſagacious Petty, and
the experienced Child, the profound Temple, and
the intelligent Davenant, had all taken it for granted, as a poſtulate which could not be diſputed, *that
a balance of trade, either favourable or diſadvantageous, enriched or impoveriſhed every commercial
country* — a writer, as able as the ableſt of them,
ſhould have at length appeared, who denied the
truth of its exiſtence, at leaſt of its efficacy! The
late Mr. Hume ſeems to have written his fine
Eſſay on the Balance of Trade, partly with deſign
to throw a diſcredit on the declamations of Mr.
Gee, " *which had ſtruck the nation with an univerſal
panic,*" perhaps more with the laudable purpoſe of
convincing the public " *of the impoſſibility of our
loſing our money by a wrong balance, as long as we
preſerve our people and our induſtry.*"

Whatever wiſe men may determine with regard
to this curious, perhaps important ſpeculation,
reaſon mean while aſſerts, what experience ſeems
to confirm, " *that there is a certain quantity of bullion ſent by one nation to another, to pay for what
they have not been able to compenſate by the barter
of commodities, or by the remittance of bills of ex-*
change

change; which may be therefore deemed the balance of trade." And a writer on political œconomy, equal to Mr. Hume in reach of capacity, and superior to him in accuracy of argument, the late Sir James Stewart, has examined his reasonings, and overturned his fyftem, elegant in its ftructure, but weak in its foundation. It behoves us, therefore, to look a little more narrowly into the ftate of the traffic which Britain carries on with the world, in order to difcover, if poffible, how much bullion fhe pays to each of her commercial correfpondents, or how much fhe receives from them.

Admitting that the apparent tide of payments flowed againft this ifland anterior to the Revolution, it does not feem eafy to difcover the exact point of time when it began to ebb in a contrary direction.

Sir Philip Meadows, we have feen, found a balance in our favour, on an average of the bufinefs of 1694 —5—6, of   —   —   *£.* 74,000.

The ledger of the infpector-general fhewed a balance, on the traffic of 1697, of   —   —   —   43,341.

The re-eftablifhment of peace gave us a return, in 1698, of   —   1,789,744.

But, an increafe of imports reduced the balance, in 1699, to   —   1,080,497.

And an augmentation of exports again raifed the balance, in 1700, to   —   —   —   1,332,541.

We

We now behold the dawn of knowledge, in respect to this interesting part of our œconomy, which has at all times been the most enveloped in darkness, which sometimes introduced all the unpleasantness of uncertainty, and entailed too often the gloom of despondence, But, it ought to be remembered, that whether we import more than we export, is a mere question of fact, which depends on no one's opinion, since, like all other disputable facts, it may be proved by evidence.

We must recur once more to the ledger of the inspector-general of our foreign trade, as the best evidence which the nature of the inquiry can furnish, or perhaps ought to be required. After admitting the force of every objection that has been made against the entries at the custom-house, we may apply to that curious record of our traffic, what the Lord Chief Justice Hale * asserted, with regard to the parish registers of births and burials, *" that it gives a greater demonstration than a hundred notional arguments can either evince or confute."* It was from that source of accurate information, that the balances were drawn which are inserted in the foregoing chronological table : and it requires only *" a snatch of sight "* to perceive all the fluctuations of our mercantile dealings with the world, as they were directed by our activity, or our caprice, or remissness, and to decide with regard to the extent of our gains at every period, by the settlement of our grand account of profit and loss on every commercial adventure. One

* Origin of Mankind, p. 207.

truth

truth muſt be admitted, which has been conſidered
by ſome as a melancholy one, becauſe they inferred from it, " *that we were driving a loſing
trade*," that the apparent balance has been leſs
favourable in the preſent than in the preceding
reign. In order to account for this unwelcome
notice, it has been inſiſted, that, as we grew more
opulent, we became more luxurious, and, as our
voluptuouſneſs increaſed, our induſtry diminiſhed,
till, in the progreſs of our folly, we found a delight in ſacrificing our diligence and œconomy to
the gratifications of a pleaſurable moment, dur-
ring a diſſipated age.

But, declamation is oftener uſed to conceal the
bewitching errors of ſophiſtry, than to inveſtigate
the inſtructive deductions of truth. Conſidering
the balance of trade as an intereſting ſubject to a
commercial nation, it muſt be deemed not only
of uſe, but of importance, to enquire minutely
which of our mercantile correſpondents are our
debtors, and which are our creditors ; and to ſtate
which country remits us a favourable balance, and
to which we are obliged in our turn to pay one.
Nor, is it ſatisfactory to contraſt the general balances of different periods, in order to form general concluſions, which may be either juſt or falla-
cious, as circumſtances are attended to or neglected.
From a particular ſtatement it will clearly appear,
that we trade with the greater number of the nations of Europe on an advantageous ground ; with
few of them on an unfavourable one ; that ſome
ſtates, as Italy, Turkey, and Venice, may be conſidered

fidered as of a doubtful kind, becaufe they are not, in their balances, either conftantly favourable or unfavourable. To banifh uncertainty from dif-quifition is always of importance. With this de-fign, it is propofed to ftate an average of the ba-lance of apparent payments, which were made during the years 1771—2—3 to England by each correfponding community, or which fhe made to them: and the averages of thefe years are taken, in order to difcover the genuine balance of trade on the whole, fince they feemed to be the leaft affected by the approaching ftorm. Where the feale of remittance vibrates in fufpence, between the countries of doubtful payments, an average of fix years is taken, deducting the adverfe exceffes of import and of export from each other.

Let us examine the following detail of our Eu-ropean commerce:

Countries of favourable balances			Countries of unfavourable balances.		
Denmark and Norway —	£.	78,478	Eaft country [doubtful]	£.	100,230
Flanders —	—	780,088	Ruffia —	—	822,607
France —	—	190,605	Sweden —	—	117,365
Germany —	—	695,484	Turkey [doubtful]	—	120,497
Holland —	—	1,464,149	Venice [doubtful] —	—	11,369
Italy [doubtful] —		43,289			
Portugal } —	—	274,132		£.	1,172,068
Madeira } —	—	9,514	Favourable balance		3,636,504
Spain } —	—	442,539			
Canaries } —	—	23,347			
Streights —	—	113,310			
Ireland —	—	663,516			
Ifle of Man —	—	13,773			
Alderney —	—	1,229			
Guernfey [doubtful] —		6,269			
Jerfey [doubtful] —		8,850			
	£.	4,808,572		£.	4,808,572

Having

Having thus fairly ftated the countries of Europe, from which we receive yearly a balance on our trade, againft thofe to which we annually make unfavourable payments ; and having found, upon ftriking the difference, that we gained, at the commencement of the prefent war, a nett balance of £. 3,636,504, let us now enquire what we gained or loft by *our factories* in Africa and in Afia.

Africa — — £. 656,599		Eaft Indies — £. 1,105,511	
Unfavourable balance 448,912			
£. 1,105,511		£. 1,105,511	

Having thus found an unfavourable balance on the traffic of our factories, of £. 448,912, it is now time to examine the trade of our then colonies, which has too often been confidered as the only commerce worthy of our care; as if we had gained every thing, and loft nothing by it.

Favourable balances.		Unfavourable balances.	
Newfoundland [doubtful] £. 29,484	Antigua — —£. 44,168		
Canada — — 187,974	Barbadoes — — 44,969		
Nova Scotia — — 34,434	Carolina [doubtful] — 108,050		
New England — — 790,244	Hudfon's Bay — — 2,501		
New York — — 343,992	Jamaica — 753,770		
Penfylvania — — 521,900	Montferrat — — 46,623		
Virginia and } — 165,230	Nevis — — 47,238		
Maryland [doubtful] }	St. Chriftopher's — 149,259		
Georgia [doubtful] — 360	Grenades — — 288,362		
Florida — — 37,966	Dominica — — 158,447		
Bermudas — — 9,541	St. Vincent — — 104,238		
	Tobago — — 16,064		
£. 2,121,125	New Providence — 2,094		
	Tortola — — 23,032		
	St. Croix — — 11,697		
	St. Euftatia — — 5,096		
	Spanifh Weft Indies — 35,352		
	Greenland — — 18,274		
	Balance — 261,291		
£. 2,121,125	£. 2,121,125		

Let

Let us now recapitulate the foregoing balances!

Gained on our European commerce —	£. 3,636,504
Deduct the loss on the trade of our factories —	448,912
	£. 3,187,596
Gained on the balance of our colony commerce —	261,291
Nett balance gained on the trade of England	£. 3,448,887
Nett balance gained on the trade of Scotland, according to an average of 1771—2—3 —	435,957
Nett gain on the British commerce —	£. 3,884,844

Of an extensive building, we vainly attempt to form an accurate judgment, of the proportion of the parts, or the beauty of the whole, without measuring the size of the columns, and examining the congruity of the result, by the suitableness of every dimension. Of the British commerce, so luxuriant in its shoots, and so interwoven in its branches, it is equally impossible to discover the total or relative products, without calculating the gain or loss, that ultimately results to the nation from every market. Thus, in the foregoing statement we perceive, which of our European customers pay us a balance, favourable and constant; which of them are sometimes our debtors, and at other times our creditors; which of them continually draw an unfavourable balance from us: and, by opposing the averages of the profits and losses of every annual adventure to each other, we at length discovered, from the result, the vast amount of our gains. The mercantile transactions at our factories in Africa and Asia, were stated

7   against

againſt each other, becauſe they ſeemed to be of a
ſimilar nature. But, whether we ought to conſider
the balance of £. 448,912 as abſolutely loſt, muſt
depend on the eſſential circumſtance, whether we
conſume at home the merchandizes of the Eaſt,
or, by exporting them for the conſumption of
ſtrangers, we draw back with intereſt what we had
only advanced : ſhould the nation prefer the beau-
tiful manufactures of the Indian to her own, we
ought to regard her prudence as on a level with
the indiſcretion of the milliner, who adorns her
own perſon with the gaudy attire, which ſhe had
prepared for the ornament of the great and the gay.
Our then colonies were ſtated againſt each other,
in order to ſhew the relative advantage of each,
as well as the real importance of the whole. Of
the valuable products imported from them, which
ſeem to form ſo great a balance againſt the nation,
we ought to obſerve, that they are either gainful,
or diſadvantageous, as we apply them: we gain
by the tobacco, the ſugars, the ſpirits, the drugs,
the dying-woods, which we re-export to our neighbours: we loſe by what we unneceſſarily waſte.

The colony war has added greatly to our ancient ſtock of experience, by exhibiting the ſtate
of our commerce in various lights, as it was forced
into different channels. The balance of trade has
thence aſſumed a new appearance, as it is ſhewn
by the cuſtom-houſe books. While the exports
were depreſſed for a time, as they had been ſtill
more by former wars, the imports roſe in the ſame
proportion.

proportion. The value of both, from England,
were,

	Exports.	Imports.
in 1781 —	£. 10,569,187 —	£. 11,918,991
82 —	12,355,750 —	9,532,607
83 —	13,851,671 —	12,114,644
84 —	14,171,375 —	14,119,166

The number of ships, which, during these years,
entered inwards, have also increased fully equal to
the augmented value of cargoes. But, were we
to form a judgment of the balance of trade from
the difference which thus appears from the custom-
house books, we should be led to manifest error.
Let us take the year 1784 for an example. Thus
stood

	Exports.	Imports.	Balance.
The East India trade	£.730,858	£.2,996,548	£.2,265,690
The West India trade —	1,160,070 —	3,372,785 —	2,212,715
The Greenland trade —	—	54,050 —	54,050
	£.1,890,928	£.6,423,383	£.4,532,455

Yet, this £.4,532,455, consisting of the importations from our factories, our colonies, and fishery,
forms no legitimate balance, however much this
vast sum may deduct from the apparent balance of
the custom-house account. The same statement,
and the same observation, may be made with regard to the trade of Scotland. To this may
be added, a melancholy truth, that we have lost
the export of corn, to the annual value of a million, which is said to be owing rather to an increase

creafe of people, than to a decline of agriculture,
and which entered with fo much advantage into
the balance of 1749—50—51. In years of fcarcity we now import large quantities of corn; and
when fo great a fum is taken from the one fcale,
and thrown into the other, the difference on the
apparent balance muft neceffarily be immenfe.

Of the truth of thefe reafonings, and of thefe
facts, the general exchanges, which are univerfally
admitted to have been, for fome years, extremely
favourable to Great Britain, are a fufficient confirmation. When there exifts no diforder in the
coin, the exchange is no bad teft, though it is
no abfolute proof on which fide the balance of
payments turns, whether againft a commercial
country, or for it. The vaft importations of foreign coin and bullion, fince the eftablifhment of
peace, prove how much and how generally the
exchanges had run in favour of this enterprizing
nation. And the price of bullion, which, during
this period, has been much lower than had ever
been known, leads us to infer, that the extent of
thefe importations has been proportionally great.

In confidering the balance of trade, it is to be
lamented, that we cannot obtain, from the tonnage of veffels entering inwards, the fame fatif-
factory information, as we have already gained
from the numbers of fhipping, which having carried out the merchandizes, were brought as a
confirmation of the value of exported cargoes:
for, the materials of. manufacture, being much
bulkier than the manufactures themfelves, require

Q   a greater

a greater number of tranfports. It may, however, give a new view of an engaging fubject, to fee the tonnage of veffels, which entered inwards at different periods, compared with the fuppofed balance of trade.

Ships cleared outwards. — 1709. — Ships entered inwards.

Tons Eng.	D° foreign.	Total.	Tons Eng.	D° foreign.	Total.
243,693 —	45,625 —	289,318	89,298 —	33,901 —	123,199
			Favourable balance of tonnage		66,119
		289,318			289,318
			Balance of merchandize fent out, exclufive of bullion —		— £. 1,402,764

Ships cleared outwards — 1718. — Ships entered inwards.

Tons Eng.	D° foreign.	Total.	Tons Eng.	D° foreign.	Total.
427,962 —	16,809 —	444,771	353,871 —	15,517 —	369,3
			Favourable balance of tonnage		
Unfavourable balance of merchandize fent out, exclufive of bullion — £. 308,000		444,771			444,771

Ships cleared outwards. — 1737. — Ships entered inwards.

Tons Eng.	D° foreign.	Total.	Tons Eng.	D° foreign.	Total.
476,941 —	26,627 —	503,568	374,593 —	45,409 —	420,002
			Favourable balance of tonnage		83,566
		503,568			503,568
			Balance of merchandize fent out, exclufive of bullion —		— £. 3,008,705

Ships

Ships cleared outwards.— 1751-2-3. —Ships entered inwards.

Tons Eng.	D° foreign.	Total.		Tons Eng.	D° foreign.	Total.
612,485	— 42,593	— 655,078		435,091	— 61,303	— 496,394
				Favourable balance of tonnage 158,684		
		655,078				655,078
				Balance of merchandise sent out, exclusive of bullion — — £. 3,976,727		

Ships cleared outwards.— 1771-2-3. —Ships entered inwards.

Tons Eng.	D° foreign.	Total.		Tons Eng.	D° foreign.	Total.
711,730	— 63,294	— 775,024		608,066	— 123,870	— 731,936
				Favourable balance of tonnage 43,088		
		775,024				775,024
				Balance of merchandise sent out, exclusive of bullion — — £. 3,518,858		

Ships cleared outwards. — 1784. — Ships entered inwards.

Tons Eng.	D° foreign.	Total.		Tons Eng.	D° foreign.	Total.
846,355	— 113,064	— 959,419		869,259	— 157,168	— 1,026,427
Unfavourable balance	—	67,008				
		1,026,427				1,026,427
Balance of merchandise sent out — — £. 52,209						

From the foregoing facts, men will probably draw their inferences, with regard to our debility and decline, or to our healthfulnefs and advancement, according to their ufual modes of thinking, to their accuftomed gloominefs or hilarity of mind, or to the effufions of the company which they commonly keep. One party, taking it for granted, amid their anxieties, that the national commerce, domeftic and foreign, is in the laft

Q 2. ftage

ftage of a confumption, may poffibly attribute a
fuppofed idlenefs and inattention to the exceffive
luxury, in kind the moft pernicious, in extent
the moft extravagant, which deeply pervades
every order : the other party, directed in their
enquiries by an habitual chearfulnefs, may perhaps determine, from the bufy occupations which
they fee in the fhop and the field, of an activity
and attention, the natural forerunners of profperity and acquifition, thinking that they perceive,
in the heavy-loaded fhips, as they arrive, *the*
materials of a manufacture, extenfive and encreaf-
ing. If any one wifhes for the aid of experience
in fixing his judgment, he need only examine the
affairs of the American States, and of Ireland,
during the effluxion of the laft hundred years.
A great balance of trade ftood conftantly againft
both thefe countries; yet, both have more than
doubled the numbers of their people, the amount
of their productive labour, the value of their exported merchandize, and the extent of their real
wealth.

From the balance of trade, which, as an interefting fubject, feemed to merit ample difcuffion, it is proper to advert to *the column of cuf-*
toms in the chronological table, becaufe we may
derive a fupplemental proof of the fucceffive increafe of our trade, of our commercial knowledge,
and of our real opulence. Thefe duties had their
commencement from the act of tonnage and
poundage, at the Reftoration, when the whole
cuftoms did not amount to £.400,000. This
law,

law, which impofed 5 per cent. of the value on
goods *exported*, as well as on goods imported, on
domeftic manufaftures, as well as on foreign merchandizes ; which laid particular taxes on *our own
woollens*, and double taxes on all goods when fent
out by aliens ; was furely framed by no very judicious plan, though two and a half per cent. of the value were allowed to be drawn back on goods, which
having been imported fhould be fent out in a twelvemonth. The publications of Mun, of Fortrey, and
of Child, foon after the Reftoration, diffufed more
univerfal acquaintance with commercial legiflation.
The alien duties on the export of native commodities and domeftic manufactures were judicioufly
repealed, in 1673 : The taxes on the exportation
of woollens, of corn, meal, and bread, were happily removed in 1700 : Yet, it was not till 1722
that, on a fyftematic confideration of burdens on
trade, all duties on the export of Britifh manufactures were withdrawn, except a few articles,
which being regarded as *materials*, were ftill to
be fent out with difcouragement. Thefe were
doubtlefs confiderable incentives to exportation,
by fending the goods fo much cheaper to market.
But the imports were difcouraged then, and have
been succeffively burdened with new fubfidies and
additional per cents. till the revenue of cuftoms fwelled to £. 3,226,639, in 1784. This fyftem admits of further improvement, which the
moft intelligent men are preparing to make. A
machine, however, of very complicated parts, re-

Q 3   quires

quires very attentive labour before it can be reduced to fewer movements of a fimpler form.

The column of coinage was introduced in the
laft place, as its proper ftation, becaufe the increafe of coins, by means of the operations of the
mint, arife generally from the profits of commerce,
at leaft from the demand of traders: and of confequence the quantity of circulating money muft
in every country be in proportion nearly to the
extent of bufinefs or frequency of transfers. The
fears of men, with regard to a wrong balance of
trade, have not been at any time greater than the
continual dread of a total deprivation of our coins.
And both have produced a numerous clafs of
writers, who have publifhed their theories, not
fo much, perhaps, to enlighten the world, as to
give vent to their lamentations.

While the rents of the land were paid in its pro-
duct; while the freemen contributed perfonal fervice inftead of a fpecified tax; and while the arts
had not yet been divided into their claffes, there
would be little ufe for the convenient meafure of
coins. The converfion of almoft every fervice
and duty into a payment of money marks a confiderable change in our domeftic affairs. And in
proportion as refinement gained ground of rude-
nefs, as induftry prevailed over idlenefs, as manufacture found its way into the nation, and as commerce extended its operations and its influence,
coins muft have become more numerous in the
fubfequent ages, becaufe they were more neceffary.
From the happy acceffion of Elizabeth, we may

trace

trace with fufficient certainty the progrefs and extent of our public coinage.

Coined by Queen Elizabeth, including the debafed filver of the three preceding reigns,	—	in gold	£. 1,200,000	
		in filver —	4,632,932	£. 5,832,932
By King James	—	in gold — £. 800,000		
		in filver —	1,700,000	2,500,000
By Charles I.	—	in gold — £. 1,723,000		
		in filver —	8,776,544	10,499,544
By the Parliament and Cromwell — in filver —			—	1,000,000
Total coined during a century, from 1558, to 1659,	— in gold — £. 3,723,000			
	in filver —	16,109,476		£. 19,832,476
Coined by Charles II.	—	— £. 7,524,105		
by James II.	—	—	2,737,637	£. 10,261,742
by William III. (including the re-coinage)	—	—		£. 10,511,983
by Anne	—	—	—	2,691,626
by George I.	—	—	—	8,725,921
by George II. from 1726 to 1760	in gold — £. 11,662,216			
	in filver —	304,360		11,966,576
Total coined during a century, from 1659 to 1760 —			—	£. 44,157,828
Coined by George III. before the 1ft January 1785	in gold — £. 33,081,884			
	in filver —	7,390		£. 33,089,274

It did not, however, efcape the penetration of
Davenant, or perhaps the fagacity of preceding
writers,—" that all this money was not co-exifting
at any one time." And he therefore endeavoured,
with his ufual induftry, to afcertain the probable
amount of our circulation, or the number of our
coins during every period, to which either his conjecture or his calculation could reach.

---

a And. Com. vol. ii. p. 105. b Ralph. Hift. vol. i. p. 1078. c Campbell's Survey. d Ibid. e Ibid. f Tower Records. g Mint account.

In

In 1600, he ſtates*, that there probably exiſted,

in gold £. 1,500,000

in ſilver 2,500,000

————————

£. 4,000,000:

which were the tools, ſaid he, *we had to work with when we firſt began to make a figure in the commercial world.*

In 1660, there were only, in all likelihood, co-ex-iſting, of every preceding coinage — £. 14,000,000. Sir William Petty †, who lived nearer the time, and had better information, aſſerts, " that the re-coinage at the happy Reſtoration amounted to £. 5,600,000; whereby it is probable (ſome allowance being given for hoarded money) that the whole caſh of England was then about £. 6,000,000; which he conceived was ſufficient to drive the trade of England."

And from the progreſs of our commerce from 1600 to 1660, and from the extent of our mer-cantile tranſactions, we may decide, which of the calculators was moſt accurate in his ſtatement, and moſt ſatisfactory in his inference. Sir Joſiah Child, indeed, remarked, in 1665‡, " *that all ſorts of men complain much of the ſcarcity of money*; yet, that men did complain as much of a ſcarcity of money ever ſince I knew the world: for, *that this humour of complaining proceeds from the frailty of our natures*, it being natural for mankind to complain of the preſent, and to commend the times paſt." That experienced merchant attributed " *the preſſing neceſſity for money, ſo viſible throughout the king-*

---

* Whit. edit. vol. i. p. 364.   † Pol. Arith. p. 278.

‡ And. Com. vol. ii. p. 142.

dom,

dom, to the trade of bankering, which obftructs circulation, and advances ufury." And from Child's State of the Nation, during feveral years fubfequent to the Reftoration, we may infer, that Petty was nearer the truth in his reprefentation than Davenant.

If the amount of our traffic, foreign and domeftic, had doubled in the active period between the Reftoration and the Revolution, we ought to conclude that the quantity of circulating coin ought to have been in the proportion of fix to twelve ; confequently,

If there had been in 1660 - - £. 6,000,000,
There ought to have been in 1688 – 12,000,000:
Yet, after a variety of *conjectures* and
calculations, Davenant ftates* it at 18,500,000;

which, he infifted, was altogether neceffary for carrying on our foreign and domeftic traffic. But, the refult of thofe conjectures, and of thofe calculations, derives little fupport, and lefs authenticity, from the facts before-mentioned ; which fhewed, that a country, which for fo many years paid confiderable balances to the world, could not abound in coins. And there was a circumftance of ftill greater weight, that feems to have been little attended to by hiftorians, or by theorifts: a rife in the intereft of money evinces a fcarcity of fpecie ; at leaft it demonftrates that the fupply is not fufficient for every demand. The *natural* intereft of

* Whit. edit. vol. i. p. 367.

money

money was eight per cent. from 1624 to 1645;
and it from this year gradually fell to six per cent.
before the Reftoration; fo that the Parliament
were enabled, in 1650, to fix by ordinance the
legal intereft at fix per cent.* ; which was confirmed by ftatute at the Reftoration †. But, the *natural*
intereft of money gradually rofe again, from fix per
cent. in 1660, to feven pounds fix fhillings and
fix pence in 1690; and from this year to feven
pounds ten fhillings per cent. before the peace of
Ryfwick. From 1697, the natural intereft of
money gradually funk, before the year 1706, to
fix per cent.; and continuing to fall, the Parliament were thereby induced [1713] to fix by
ftatute the *legal* intereft at five per cent. Yet,

In 1711, Davenant ftates, " *that there might be*
of gold and filver coin in being," to the
amount of — £. 12,000,000
In 1688, he had already found — 18,500,000

Decreafe in three and twenty years £. 6,500,000

Yet, it is highly probable, that the value of the
circulating coins might amount to £. 12,000,000
in 1711. The gradual advance of our domeftic
induftry and foreign traffic, the reform of the filver, the confequent augmentation of taxes and
circulation, the greater credit both public and private, the finking of the *natural* intereft of money;

* And. Com. vol. ii. p. 85.   † 12 Ch. II. c. 13.

all

all demonftrate the impoffibility of any diminution of our coins, during the period from the Revolution to the year 1711. Anderfon *, having
given his fuffrage to Davenant's ftatement of
1711, fays, " that we may reafonably conclude, as
our trade is confiderably increafed in fifty-one
years, the gold and filver actually exifting in Britain [1762] cannot be lefs than £. 16,000,000 :"
And we may fairly infer from the
reafonings of Anderfon, that the gold
and filver coins actually exifting now
[1786] amount to about — £. 20,000,000.

We have feen, during the prefent reign, an extraordinary augmentation of our manufactures
and our trade, a quicker transfer of property, a
vaft credit, a productive revenue, an unexampled
demand at the mint for its coins; which all evince
a greater ufe for money, and confequently a proportional fupply. And fpeculation has been actually confirmed by facts and experience. When,
by an admirable operation, a falutary reform was
made of the gold coin, there appeared fixteen million of guineas.

* Commerce, vol. ii. p. 105.

The

The three proclamations—of 1773—of 1774—
and 1776, brought in, of defective gold coin,
the value in tale of - £. 15,563,593 10 8
There moreover appeared
of guineas 'purchased by
the bank, and of light
gold which fell as a loss
on the holders of it, to
the amount * of — — 2,380,643 — —

£. 17,944,236 10 8
There remained consequently in the circle, heavy
guineas of the former
reigns and the present,
light guineas which were
not brought in, and silver £. 2,055,763 9 4

£. 20,000,000 — —

If, from the amount of the coinage of
the present reign — — 33,089,274,
the sum of light gold re-coined is deducted, — — — 15,563,594,

we shall see in the result the sum
which the increasing demand of the
present reign required at the mint,
exclusive of the re-coinage — £. 17,525,680.

* Mr. Eden's Letters, p. 215.

It

It is not eafy to difcover, becaufe data cannot
be readily found, what proportion of the coins,
which conftituted in tale this vaft balance, was afterwards melted or exported. If one-fourth only
continued in the circle of commerce, this circumftance alone, when compared with the quantity of
money which, in 1776, was actually found in circulation, would demonftrate the exiftence of a
greater number of coins, and confequently a greater
amount in tale, than has been thus evinced. One
truth is however clear, " *that every community,
which has an equivalent to give, may always procure as many of the precious metals, wherever they
may exift, as it wants;* in the fame manner as the
individual, who has labour, or any other property,
to offer in exchange, may at all times fill his coffers with medals, or with coins. Hence, we may
conclude with Mr. Hume, and with fubfequent
writers on political œconomy, equal in judgment
to him, that while we preferve our people, our
fkill, and our induftry, we may allow the fpecie to
find its own way in the world, without any other
protection than what is due to the juftnefs of our
ftandard in finenefs and weight, or without any
other care than to give continual notice to the credulous to beware of the tricks of the clipper, the
fweater, and the coiner.

SUCH

SUCH then is the eftimate of our comparative refources, of the loffes and revivals of our trade during every war, and of the numbers of our people, both before and fince the Revolution. He who has honoured the foregoing documents with an attentive perufal, may probably be induced to afk, What valid reafon is there for defpairing of the commonwealth, by relinquifhing hope ?—The individual who defponds, indulges a paffion the moft to be deplored, becaufe it is the moft incurable. The nation, which, in any conjuncture, entertains doubts of her own abilities, is already conquered, fince fhe is enflaved by her irrefolution or by her fears. The foregoing difcuffions would prove, if recent experience did not confirm the truth, that never ought we to have entertained a jufter confidence in our own powers than in the prefent moment; though no reafon, furely, exifts, for adopting expenfive projects, much lefs for running into imprudent enterprizes.

F I N I S.

INDEX.

I N D E X.

.*Edward*

R

I N D E X.

England,

I N D E X.

Gardening,

I N D E X.

INDEX.

Manufacturers,

INDEX.

I N D E X.

        Navy

I N D E X.

3   *Population*

I N D E X.

Population

INDEX.

Scotland,

I N D E X.

4

INDEX.

I N D E X.